SECRET
GARDENS
of LONDON

Caroline Clifton-Mogg
photographs by Marianne Majerus

 Thames & Hudson

*In memory of my father,
Doctor Nicolas Majerus,
who opened my eyes to the
marvels of the natural world.*

Contents

The Art of the Secret Garden   6

Country in the City   10

Outdoor Rooms   70

Classical 100

Terraces 124

Contemporary 156

The Art of the Secret Garden

Above: In Ann Mollo's garden, plants are used in harmonious compositions, sometimes of colour, sometimes of texture and shape (p. 12).
Right: A wooden bridge leads invitingly past Butia capitata *and* Cycas revoluta *into the jungle that lies beyond in Declan Buckley's North London garden (p. 90).*

London is a city of secret gardens, a place where plain-faced streets give little away of what lies there, and where few individual façades give any clues as to the secrets behind their all-embracing walls. Protected and hidden by their house the best gardens are a fusion of inside and outside. The gardens that you see in this book are a true collaboration – not only of man with nature, but also with architecture and urban planning. Whatever secret a garden may reveal, it will always surprise and delight those who discover it for the first time.

The English have long been known as a nation of gardeners. Londoners – as always, a part of the greater whole – are a sort of miniature nation of gardeners too. Blessed with a temperate microclimate, where a greater variety of plants can be grown than in other parts of the country, all horticultural tastes can be catered for and indulged.

London gardeners love to hunt and buy – to add to their stock of fine specimens; to visit the Columbia Road market on Sunday, or the many nurseries, built on valuable land scattered through the capital, or to make an annual pilgrimage to the Royal Horticultural Society's Chelsea Flower Show, where gardeners pour through the gates in their thousands. There is a profusion of enthusiasm and a knowledge here.

Of course, in any city, most of the private gardens are automatically secret. Some are secret because they are purposely hidden from view behind gates or doors; others are secret because, by the nature of their location, they are seen by invitation only; but most are secret because, even if they are one of a row of identically sized plots, no one ever quite knows what happens next door to them.

For this is a different, and widespread sort of secrecy, where what is hidden is the intent, the thoughts and plans of the gardener. A neighbour might overlook the garden of another for many years, without ever realizing that within the rectangular plot next door lies an intimate expression of one person's dream; it might be an authentic recreation of a classical Japanese landscape, or it could be a horticulturist's paradise in miniature. The borders so casually admired from over the dividing wall may in fact be a plantswoman's greatest delight and pride, with every new shoot cosseted and cajoled like the crankiest of babies, and every success celebrated with joy.

A secret garden may often be walled, but more hidden still are those built on top of buildings, for where a roof garden is open only to the sky, it may even be the most secret of them all.

All gardens start with a dream – but it is, in essence, a design, and garden design is a noble art. As well as colour and plant combinations, architecture and style also play a part, and in everything, harmony is vital because whatever the style, the final result will only be satisfactory when the different elements are in harmony with each other. Although some of the gardens in this book have been made by enthusiastic amateurs, many others have been created by professional garden designers, some of the best working in Britain today. Their innovative and imaginative

designs and ideas, ranging from the grand scale down to the perfect miniature, should inspire every one interested in the art of the garden, whether they live in a city or not.

A secret garden does not have to be solitary; it can be a retreat and a place of quiet, but it can also be a welcoming space where others can relax and unwind. But whichever category it belongs to, every proper secret garden has a personality of its own, given life by the person behind it.

This is why a garden may be hard for the outsider to fathom. No matter how many people see it, the good garden is a personal vision, a secret in the creator's mind, imagined, planned and plotted like a poem, a place where every plant combination, serpentine bed or pool of water has a meaning.

The secret gardens of London go beyond conventional form; they range from the large, classical and formal, with simple, single colour schemes, to tiny gardens that run riot with colour of every imaginable hue. There are gardens on roofs and gardens in basements, gardens where the boundaries cannot be seen and gardens on terraces. There are gardens on top of the world, gardens with water, even gardens on water. There are gardens sheltered by tropical plants, or by billowing sails. There are English cottage gardens, and modern gardens that present sculpture outdoors. There are gardens of artists and gardens of practical enthusiasts. There are artists' gardens, collectors' gardens, passionate plantsmen's gardens, gardens restored, revived or reclaimed.

The secrets revealed here – thanks to the ingenuity of London's finest garden designers, and the shared dreams of the owners of these gardens – may delight and inspire us all.

Left: in Pedro da Costa Felguieras's garden, the large sycamore tree has many uses, from acting as an oversized climbing frame for Rosa 'Bobbie James' *to providing the pollarded branches that have been used to make the charming rustic fence (p. 26).*
Above: On Michèle Osborne's roof-top garden, the lavender-filled pots are as much part of the textural composition as the octagonal, wooden decking seating area (p. 142).

Country in the City

The Collector's Garden

Holland Park, just west of Notting Hill, is a leafy, languid area of garden squares and wide avenues, dominated by the eponymous park, now public, but once the private grounds of Holland House, a mansion destroyed by a Second World War bomb.

Ann Mollo's house exudes the lazy green peace of the neighbouring park; situated, as it is, in a quiet terrace off a garden square, the façade gives no clue as to the hidden surprises both within and without. From the narrow hall to the upper attics, every room is a collector's dream, particularly if the visitor happens to be a collector of ceramics, for antique creamware is everywhere – stacked high in cupboards, on shelves and tables, jostling for space with a thousand other pretty things. Stepping gingerly through the house towards the rear, avoiding both the china and the inappropriately over-sized lurcher dog, onto a small vine-canopied iron terrace, suddenly you see the garden – an undulating stream of soft colour, with every shade of green and grey, punctuated by eddies of subtly toned pinks, whites, blues and lilacs, all meandering gently into what seems the far distance.

All this would be enchanting enough in a garden of conventional size, but what makes this garden so surprising and such a triumph is that although 55 feet (17 metres) in length (respectable for London), it is – amazingly – only 16 feet (5 metres) wide.

Into this Lilliputian space, Ann Mollo has found room for a rich and varied assortment of plants, numbered literally in the hundreds: they are mostly long-loved favourites like astrantia, aquilegia, camellia, campanula, delphinium, ferns and foxgloves; but there are also geranium and gunnera, hosta, jasmine, Solomon's seal, lilies, love-lies-bleeding, nicotiana, peonies, and of course roses, roses everywhere. Of the old roses – which are more difficult to grow than they seem – 'Russeliania' is particularly successful, flowering in abundance every year, while 'Buff Beauty' does well too.

The colour palette in this secret space is particularly English – pinks from blush to carmine, mauves and lilacs and powder-purple, cream and white and green. As so often in this sort of garden, yellow and orange and red do not appear – they would seem out of sympathy with the tenor of the garden.

Near the house stand a group of terracotta pots, most of them old and hand-thrown, each with its own, often rare, inhabitant, ranging from species

lilies to herbaceous clematis – although these last are not always entirely successful, for like all true plantswomen, Ann does admits to certain failures: 'I actually do better with the little bell clematis such as "Duchess of Albany" and "Pagoda".' There are terracotta urns too, like huge vases in an outdoor room – one is filled simply with blue lobelia, that most ubiquitous of summer bedding, but here looking like a fountain of surreally blue water as it cascades over the edges of the urn.

Half-hidden in the lushness is an old-brick path that winds up one side of the narrow plot; a sliver of lawn follows the path's serpentine contours, and on the other side shrubs and plants spill and tumble onto the green turf – which is carefully re-seeded every winter.

Everything climbs and trails in a seeming artless profusion and roses clamber over archways and pergolas, like 'Mme Isaac Pereire' which energetically climbs covers one of the arches at the end of the garden. There are three of these arches, and they act as a punctuation, breaking up the space and heralding a woodland corner, planted with favourite shade-loving plants such as ferns and hosta – these last also used to great effect elsewhere in the garden. An obelisk rises majestically, if somewhat mysteriously, out of the ferns.

There are other space-dividing devices: 'Because it is such a long plot, in order to make it appear wider, I planned it in sections that would break up the length. The idea is that you don't see everything at once, and because all the lines curve, from each point you get a different view, so much so that when you look back down from the far end the perspective is reversed and it seems like a completely different garden.'

For all its exuberance, this is not an untidy garden – there is a discipline and a structure that underlines it all, for as Ann explains, 'The shape of the garden is always here; it is just that I've planted and planted so the shape isn't obvious.'

Scattered along the length of the garden is the odd scaled-down seat – a metal chair here, a small bench there. This is a garden for contemplation and for careful study, and it is also very fragile – so much so that it is not generally opened to the public.

Ann bought the house more than forty years ago, when it was a near-derelict workman's cottage with a so-called garden that contained little other than an

Above: in a quiet spot that could almost be woodland, a white-painted chair amid ferns and ivy. Left: lilies, hosta and an unusual Hydrangea arborescens *'Annabelle', surround the arbour. Following pages: looking down into the richness of the garden from the small, vine-laden terrace that leads from the house, is a table for coffee and drinks, with low urns filled with hostas, 'Hadspen Blue' and 'Halcyon'.*

air-raid shelter, several old gas cookers and some slabs of concrete. So – as with all the best secret gardens – she had to start from scratch.

She was then a novice gardener, learning as she went. And the more she learnt, the more fascinated she became, until her fascination developed, as she now admits, into an addiction.

'I love plants and I love country gardens and that's what this is – well, as close as I can get to it, anyway. The garden has evolved as I have evolved, and of course over time my tastes have changed and I now love things like hostas which at the beginning, I didn't like at all. In the beds I grow lilies like *Lilium Casa Blanca* and *Lilium regale* 'Album' – that most beloved of lilies – and then I grow lilies in pots like *Lilium cernuum* and other more obscure bulbs.

'My pleasure comes from the minute appreciation of each plant. I love to see them opening.' As far as the selection of plants goes, she tries everything – 'If you lose things, you lose them; it used to worry me, but now I know you have to face the facts.'

Ann has now acquired the derelict, untended garden next door – this secret garden may prolong the collector's dream for some time to come.

Above: a place for contemplation. Urns filled with hosta 'Hadspen Blue' are off-set with tumbling pelargoniums.
Left: the arbour, with a seat from which to survey the beauty around It is almost impossible to comprehend that although 55 feet (17 metres long), the whole garden is only 16 feet (5 metres) wide.

Impressions of Japan

*Above: a paper bark maple (*Acer griseum*) in early spring. Right: what seems to be a traditional, enchanted Japanese landscape, complete with larch tree and mountain stream, is in fact part of the Japanese garden designed by Peter Sievert for his London home. Every detail is reproduced in miniature perfection.*

Like many large cities today, London was originally a cluster of villages – and many would say it still is. But as it has spread ever outwards, some real villages have survived within the enclaves of what is now known as Greater London. Enfield, to the north of the city, is one of these. Woodland, parks and rides surround the area, and the small road in which Peter Sievert lives could easily be many, many miles further out of town.

So through the glass doors at one end of the sitting room, it is particularly surprising to see a scene that could almost be out of a book of Japanese prints. There is a rounded and clipped mountain pine, a rushing, tumbling stream, and age-worn rocks and boulders. And there are other trees besides – a maple with its delicate star-like leaves, a gnarled oak (grown from an acorn) and a spiky-tailed larch – all exact and perfect and in miniature. This is no pastiche of a Japanese garden, it is the real thing, with mature trees, thirty years old and 10 or 15 feet (3 or 4 metres) high, and in truth not much imagination is needed to see it as a true landscape.

Peter Sievert is a 'semi-retired' landscape gardener, and his interest in Japanese gardens dates back thirty years. He laid out this garden about twenty-three years ago – although it didn't start out in quite the same manner. 'My girlfriend doesn't go for all things Japanese; she would have preferred a design that looked like a Welsh valley, so I began to lay that out, but I surreptitiously added a few Japanese elements along the way.' Not that he feels the traditional Japanese garden is in fact that far removed from the landscape of Wales, or the Lake District or even Cornwall – 'in all those places, the native landscape has elements that are similar to those in a stylized Japanese garden.'

What appeals to him is the idea of trying to bring a certain type of idealized landscape into his own garden. Since mountainous areas are the landscapes he loves best, he has endeavoured to create in this very small space – 15 by 30 feet

(4.5 by 9 metres) – the natural features of a uplands garden, with a tumbling highland stream rather than lazy lowland water, and the rockwork representing the massive, fallen stones found towards a mountain's peak. (The boulders, in fact – all eight tons of them – were hauled by Peter all the way from the wilds of North Wales.)

The design of such a garden is vital. 'In many ways the illusion tends to be lost when you walk into it, because it's not meant to be a garden in the under-

Below: this perfectly clipped, aged oak – Quercus robur – has been grown over time, trained and carefully positioned to look as though it has spent its natural life in the mountains of Japan.

Right: carefully chosen moss-covered stones, and ferns growing around the traditional wooden water feature. Following pages: A larch stretches over the stream fed by a miniature waterfall.

stood sense, but a piece of landscape, so what is important is where you're going to place your rocks and where the trees should go.' There are some useful visual tricks known to designers of Japanese gardens, such as planting the tallest trees in the foreground, with trees of diminishing heights planted towards the rear – the false perspective adds to the illusion of distance. Shrubs too can be treated in the same manner, with the larger-leafed specimens planted in front of small-leafed specimens, leading one to believe that those furthest away are actually the same size as those nearest to you.

Obviously, with this style of garden, the pruning and clipping of the trees into shape is all-important, and Peter's has learnt how to do it as well as he does through a combination of research during visits to Japan and practical experiment, learning to clip the trees not through books (there are few authoritative ones in English) but through practising on miniature bonsai trees. The pine is particularly wonderful and Peter treasures it. 'They are common in Japanese gardens but oddly, its one area where I think we beat them: our Scots Pine both trains and looks better than their Red Pine.'

Colour in the garden is not a consideration. 'I don't go out of my way to introduce colour – it's the overall effect that counts in a garden like this and that should be predominantly green. There is colour in the trees, and there also is some seasonal colour – from plants like pieris and the primulas that seed themselves.'

This is important because in a traditional Japanese garden, the number of species should be low. 'I've tried to keep to that rule but it's very difficult not to overplant. I have heard it said that a Japanese garden is not complete until there is nothing more you can take out of it.'

Peter Sievert gives the impression that to create – and maintain – such a garden is easy – but although that can hardly be the case, he does find working here a source of relaxation. 'Even when I was working full time, constructing other people's gardens, I loved to come home and clip and prune; there is no digging to be done, and if you do make mistakes in the shaping of the trees, you are able to rectify them over years rather than weeks. Probably time and patience are the most important things you can bring to a Japanese garden.' The peace and calm beauty of this miniature landscape is ample testament.

Portuguese Pleasure Garden

Above: a perfect Sleeping Beauty, secret garden rose – 'Comtesse de Murinais'. Right: the pollarded sycamore at the end of the garden acts as a frame for a vigorous Rosa *'Bobbie James' climbing into its branches; below is a floral feast which includes delphiniums, poppies, lilies and* Rosa *'Königin von Dänemark'.*

Pedro da Costa Felguieras never thought he was a gardener until one day he began to take notice of what was around him. An artist, and originally from Portugal, he came to England fourteen years ago and now specializes in restoring old lacquer furniture and designing and making new pieces.

Pedro's first home in London was an upper-floor flat near the Columbia Road street market, famous for its plants – and so he began to buy small pots to keep on the window sills and balcony.

His next move, to where he now lives, was to a first-floor flat in a housing association conversion in North London, and for some time after he moved there, although able to look down onto it, he had no access to the untended garden below. But the housing association decided that there should be a fire escape staircase from the first to ground floor – that is to say, leading from his kitchen down to the garden – and so suddenly, presto, he was a gardener.

The first thing Pedro did was to target the large sycamore at the end of the garden, pollarding its heavy branches – a task he now does annually, climbing up it in the winter and taking out any overhanging growth. The pollarded sycamore has actually become almost an element of the design, as the space around its roots is used as a base for autumn and spring flowering bulbs such as cyclamen and fritillary, and through its truncated branches a very vigorous rose – 'Bobbie James' – happily grows. On the end wall behind the sycamore is a lacquered panel, designed and made by Pedro, that acts as a reflective background and which distracts attention from the gardens and houses behind. Neither is the cut sycamore wood wasted – on one side of the garden is a pretty open-work fence, like a rustic trellis, that Pedro made from some of the branches; it is much-liked by his neighbour.

This ability to recycle and use available materials is also evident in the rest of the garden. 'I used what I could find. The water butt was found in a skip –

Right:
the paper-like
petals of the
opium poppy,
here grown for its
visual qualities.

Below: Looking back towards
the house, the brick-paved
terrace surrounded by opium
poppies and Rosa 'Königin
von Dänemark', as well as
ornamental vegetables.

and the brick paving, for example, which is very pretty, also came from a skip, or rather several skips.' He kept the paved area in the centre relatively small as he didn't want paving to take up planting space – 'I wanted as much space as possible for my plants.' Interestingly, the bricks are not pointed – each one sits squarely on the soil and he has introduced camomile plants between some and moss has introduced itself between others. And if a brick should come out of place – well, 'It's easy enough to replace one brick.'

Pedro may have been new to gardening but one thing he did know was that he wanted roses, which he ordered from David Austin, the great English rose grower. He likes them full, and he likes them big – he doesn't like to see earth at all, so at the moment flowers include enormous sunflowers, anemone, in the autumn cyclamen, and in the spring, fritillaries.

In a small garden like Pedro's, scent is important. 'There are the roses of course, and also plants like nicotiana, and when it's a hot day you come down and smell all the flowers. If it weren't for scent, any garden would be just so much plastic.' But there are not only flowers; being a good Portuguese, Pedro knew that he must have vegetables, so he decided to grow those as well, wherever he could find a place in the garden.

It was not too difficult to decide what vegetables to grow – the perky fronds of cavolo nero stand up between the flowers, amd there are tomatoes, rocket, pumpkins, rhubarb and beans. 'I love growing vegetables – they are so decorative and pretty, but, of course I'm scared of eating them because then they'll leave a gap.'

This doesn't mean he isn't tempted – the leaves of the cavolo nero are picked off to make authentic *caldo verde* soup, and the spaghetti squash is used every year to make delicious jam. It all reminds him of Portugal. This combination of vegetables and flowers also means that there are enough skeletal forms to see it through the winter, to give the garden bones in fact.

'There was no grand plan,' he says, 'and there still isn't. Like all good gardens it evolves and changes all the time and for me it is always a joy and a pleasure.' Spoken like a true gardener.

Mile End Restored

Above: the dramatic iron gate with its brick piers surmounted by eagles is in fact new, re-created by Todd Longstaffe-Gowan as a suitably grand entrance for this 18th-century house. Right: the back garden of the house is a calm, peaceful and shady retreat dominated by massive tree ferns that tower up to window level.

O n the busy Mile End Road, through a handsome tall iron gate in a brick wall, you can see Malplaquet House, a double-fronted merchant's house set in a lush front garden of almost tropical exuberance. Built in 1741, its imposing façade is a reminder of the importance, in the 17th and 18th centuries, of what is now known as the East End. Then the area was the very heart of London, and rich merchant princes, their fortunes made through trading, built imposing mansions that reflected their grandeur and riches.

By the time Todd Longstaffe-Gowan and Tim Knox found Malplaquet House, it had long been empty – it was, in fact, due for demolition before it was acquired by the Spitalfields Trust, a charitable organization which rescues architecturally important houses in the area and finds people who are prepared to restore and renovate them. Malplaquet's last incarnation had been as light industrial premises, housing a printer and a typewriter repair shop with single-storey shop fronts built in front of the façade, filling the basement and obliterating what was once the front garden. There was, to put it mildly, some work to be done.

Fortunately, Todd Longstaffe-Gowan is a noted landscape designer, and Tim Knox is Head Curator of the National Trust; between them they were able to see the promise that lay beneath the ruin and rubble. By the end of 1999, they managed to get the shop fronts in front of the house demolished and suddenly before them stood the magnificent façade – albeit in very sorry state. 'When we had taken the shops down there was literally nothing there and we obviously had a very deep area to fill, so we began by bringing in completely new top soil and filled it to a depth of 5 feet [1.5 metres] or so.' Miraculously, the original front door was found beneath the rubble and they were able to recreate the surround, and build steps and paths, using traditional materials like Portland stone, 'so that now it is quite like how it was in the 18th century,' says Todd. High walls were built, and a handsome iron gate forged from old iron. 'I love high walls. The Mile End Road is busy, busy, and I wanted to literally shut it out – at least visually. I wanted to achieve a feeling of enclosure rather than opening out.' But Todd also wanted to retain the character and some of the house's history, so the dividing wall of the garden, with its traces of 19th century printers' marks and original paint colour, was kept intact, and glimpses can be seen behind the riot of vegetation which now fills the space.

At first sight today, the front garden, once so sad, appears like a jungle in its exuberance, boasting a couple of palm trees, a flourishing olive, myrtle,

roses and bay and euphorbia. 'I just can't resist growing more and more out here.'

There are climbers of every description, on the walls including clematis and a wisteria that has raced 40 feet (12 metres) in three years; it will soon start to cover the railings that run the length of the party wall. 'The garden is supposed to be an evocation of what I like and what I like is all things eclectic and idiosyncratic. It is my own little jungle really; it wasn't meant to be particularly tropical, but I was brought up in the tropical West Indies so perhaps those are my leanings; also there is a very good southern exposure on this side of the house.'

As in a Roman garden there are pots everywhere – on the steps filled with agapanthus, herbs and grasses, and continuing through the garden as well as

round the edges of the front area. The area is deep, taking up the original cellar space, and down in the reclaimed basement dining room, you look from the window up towards plants and more plants – all of which give a pleasing, watery green glow to the room. From the kitchen you look out onto a cheery sea of green herbs and colourful annuals; every window has possibilities – every window brings one or both of the gardens in. In fact the whole garden has been partially designed to be seen from the house, for as you climb the stairs, from every window you look down onto a mass of pleasing vegetation – a 'tapestry of texture,' as Todd puts it.

The north-facing back garden is about 40 feet wide and 25 feet deep (12 metres by 7.5 metres), surrounded by 14 foot (4 metre) high walls; it was once an enormous 18th-century manorial garden. In sharp contrast to the exuberant front garden, this is a cool, quiet place, dominated by ferns, both ordinary, and some particular – tree ferns brought in under special licence from New Zealand, including one or two that are at least 300 years old. There are also other plants – clematis, kiwi fruit, rose, wisteria and climbing hydrangea – but the overall impression is one of deep green-ness. 'There are ephemeral colours in spring, but basically I go for leaf texture and shape; I wanted it to be like an Italian courtyard garden, a retreat.' From the house you look down onto an exotic sea of the tops of crowns. 'I like outsize things in a small space; sometimes it looks almost primeval, although it is not supposed to evoke any particular period.'

Here, on paving stones, are a table and chairs for summer eating; the garden is not lit, candles only are used. A cobbled path, made from recycled building site cast-offs, leads mysteriously into the undergrowth, going nowhere in particular.

There are plans, next year, for a watery rockwork on the back wall, planted with ferns. There will be change, and it will continue, for these gardens are definitely still a work in progress.

Left: in the north-facing back garden, the charms of colour have given way to an exercise in green, tone, shape and texture; the picture is completed by the dramatic tree ferns, some more than 300 years old. Above: the aim with this garden was to make it a retreat, with the cool air of an Italian courtyard: a place for repose and rest.

Left: on the steps leading up to the front door, terracotta pots are filled, Mediterranean-style, with any number of plants – agapanthus, herbs and grasses.

Below left: striking in its design is this pot filled not with plants, but with elk and deer antlers.

Right: the front garden is a story of tropical jungle run riot. Exuberance abounds with palms, an olive, as well as Melianthus major, Trachycarpus fortunei, Angelica archangelica, Echium pininana, *with* Rosa *'Buff Beauty' climbing through all it comes across.*

Following pages: Hard to imagine that this peaceful scene is in the middle of the East End of London; in the back garden, towering tree ferns frame a white-clothed table and chairs.

The Artist's Garden

Above: by a raised bed is a sculpture by Camilla Shivarg framed by a tree fern, fronds of Miscanthus sacchariflorus *and* Aralia elata *'Aureovariegata'.*
Right: Vitis coignetiae *climbs up against a wall, and* Melianthus major *is reflected in the pool. The fountain is a 'Green Man' mask, by Camilla Shivarg. Following pages: a view of the garden, showing the steps that lead up to the second terrace, a curved lawn into which plants tumble in abundance.*

Some of the most interesting gardens are those that belong to artists. Camilla Shivarg is a sculptor and a painter and her garden on the Earl's Court Road in West London is a testament to her painterly eye. This itself is quite remarkable, since the Earl's Court Road is one of London's busiest cross-routes and subject to more carbon monoxide, dirt and general traffic than one would wish for a garden. Still, plants don't seem to mind – Camilla's plants are large and bouncing with life, which is hardly surprising, considering the amount of care and attention she lavishes upon them. Indeed, so fond is she of her plants that she even concocts individual mixtures of nutrients for each one.

This high maintenance aspect of gardening does not trouble her: 'I have always been a very keen gardener – it's just always been there. My grandmother was very keen and that's where it began. I am a plantswoman; in this garden, I wanted as many plants as possible, and my husband wanted a lawn, and this is the result.' It is a pretty, quite shady, garden, and fairly deep for London, measuring about 70 feet by 25 feet (21 by 7.5 metres), designed as a series of gentle terraces with a circular lawn on the second terrace, and every space crammed with plants, shrubs, colour and shape, for she is as she puts it 'a compulsive shopper, buying new things every year.' Interspersed with the planting throughout the garden are Camilla's sculptures, integral parts of the overall design.

The terraces are a clever and very effective way of improving a garden that is long and flat – a typical London garden in fact – as they give an immediate sense of perspective and subtle depth. The plants – of which more can be planted in a terrace garden – can be seen more clearly and the drainage is better. However, such dense planting can bring problems. 'Some of the beds against the wall are just too shallow, which means a lot of feeding, so I mulch everything – and use wonderful water gel crystals which look like chopped up rock sea salt. When you put water on them they expand and hold the water in the ground.'

'We wanted a theme of circles, and to include within those circles the lawn and the pond as well.' Ah, the pond – this small pool seems to be a breeding ground for more goldfish than must exist at the London Aquarium, for in its depths are fish of every size, some as small and bright as glow worms, others larger, like little bolsters of burnished gold.

At the end of the garden is a fairly new and rather complicated trellis structure designed around a mirror which reflects back and enlarges the garden. It replaces various rubbish heaps: 'When we bought the garden there was, at this end, a huge compost heap which apparently sheltered some dead cats – we searched through the whole thing, but found no dead cats, which was a shame, because I was looking forward to finding cats' skulls.'

The plants that thrive here generally do well in shady gardens, like pansies, violas, and begonia: 'I can't grow the more obvious English garden plants like lupins or delphiniums – they just don't flourish.' As you might expect Camilla grows unusual and interesting plants here, like the *Cercis canadensis* 'Forest Pansy', and a classy dark scabious – 'Chile Black'. A mound of what looked like pretty spreading, miniature rose turns out, surprisingly, to be a double variety of that often disdained creature the Busy Lizzy. In a corner there is the bleach plant brought back from Tangier, *farfugium*, as well as equisetum, also known as mare's tail. There is also an unusual annual, *Persicaria* 'Red Dragon', as well as a wonderful deep purple salvia, 'Purple Emperor'.

There is not a lot of forward planning in all this: 'I can't do it like that; I just go round and place it. I am an adherent of the "have to do it wrong to get it right" school. It was Vita Sackville-West who advocated going round the garden with a pot and just trying it to see how it goes. If it's happy, then it stays, and basically everything is doing well because hopefully it is in the right spot and looked after. I check them all the time, and I like to raise seedlings – and weedlings – first hunting them out and then moving, or removing, them. '

The colours combinations, as you might expect of an artist, are subtle and interesting. 'There is a lot of yellow in the garden, including a golden yellow bed, which is surprising, because I wouldn't have called myself a yellow person, but in the shade, yellow lifts everything, so I've quite come round to it.'

But no garden is static, and just because this garden is bursting with colourful life does not mean that Camilla can relax – 'One musn't get complacent. Look at that tree fern, that needs work – and that huge eight-leafed buddleia, I must do something about that…' It is obviously true that for a real gardener the end is never in sight.

Above: an unusual and delicate combination of shape and texture, composed of plants such as Canna *'Durban',* Ricinus communis, Verbascum *'Jackie',* Achillea *'Terracotta' and* phormium. *Left: Positioned against a wall, like the god of the garden and surrounded by one of the prettiest and most unusual of* Abutilon *('Kentish Belle'), is one of Camilla Shivarg's enigmatic sculptures.*

Below: The far end of the garden is dark and shady. Several light-enhancing and dramatic devices relieve the gloom, including the always effective device of a mirror in the furthest corner, reflecting light back into the garden.

Left: further along the end wall, the garden is designed to add interest to the darkest area. Wooden trellis and works of sculpture by Camilla Shivarg jostle with plants of dramatic shape – like plume poppy, cordyline, and Asparagus densiflorus 'Sprengeri Group'.

South London Sanctuary

Above: looking back into artist and designer Susan Collier's conservatory, where the brightly patterned curtain is made from one of her textile designs. The terrace is just as colourful, with hydrangea and pelargonium in containers, as well as borders designed to add still more colour. Right: inside the conservatory, pots of brightly coloured pelargoniums lead the eye out to the garden – a mass of continually changing colour, helped by the many varieties planted, including hydrangeas, roses, and Eupatorium.

*J*ust as Paris may be divided into Left and Right Bank, London is divided both physically and spiritually by the River Thames, and the majority of city dwellers are firmly loyal to one side or the other, 'north of the river' or 'south of the river'. Susan Collier, the well known textile designer, has always been a 'south-of-the-river' person, and the area in which she now lives boasts quiet streets, comfortable rather than remarkable houses, and long, green gardens.

Often in a city a secret garden can even be a secret to its owner, and Susan Collier's garden is a case in point. When, five years ago, she unwillingly left her much loved old house in a very picturesque part of South London, she bought this less pretty, less charming new house, almost on the rebound, as she herself admits, and only really because it had a separate studio where she could work. The basic garden such as it was – long and fairly narrow – played no part in her rather reluctant decision.

The first year, she spent, as she puts it, 'sulking' – still filled with regrets about her previous house and unwilling to do much to the new one, either inside or out. At the end of a year, however, the statutory mourning period over, she looked outside the window, started to think about what best to do – and began to dig: 'Action is a good way to recover, and making something pretty is great solace for the soul.'

The first thing she did was to take out much of the existing planting – what she calls 'horrible navy-blue plants', by which she means those which were neat, well-behaved but basically boring. Then she started planting new plants that she bought and old specimens that she had brought with her, like euphorbia, iris and astilbe. The planting itself was easier than she expected: 'This garden grows fantastically well. Things seem to literally jump up out of the ground, because the earth itself is very good – the result, I think, of generations of keen gardeners making and using compost'.

The garden is best entered through the Edwardian conservatory which, with its multi-coloured stained glass panes, seems to set the tone for the brightness beyond.

48

*No space is wasted
in Susan Collier's
garden; the
conservatory
is pressed into use
as a place to grow
grapes, as well as to
store a varied collection
of terracotta pots.*

*Below: a place
in the garden to
eat and drink; the
ground has been paved.
The table is made of
terracotta mosaic. Green
painted bamboo poles form
a lightweight arbour and
nasturtiums climb upwards.*

Susan is first and foremost an artist and therefore the garden she began to create had to be one of colour and contour, a palette of tones and shades, and contrast of shape and form. Colour has always been Susan's signature, and as one might imagine, her horticultural colour combinations are striking and original – areas of strong, vibrant colour contrasting with drifts of pastel tones.

In this informal garden – so informal that it seems, in some places, to be verging on the wild – a central gravel path leads down through several contrasting areas. Susan has divided the space into three small separate sections, and that nearest the house – which she wanted to be an instant surprise to those venturing out – features perennials, separated by the path into two borders of completely contrasting palettes: to the right an assertive bank of sunshine yellow, orange and red, to the left a wave of subtle blues and lilacs. Like many an artist, Susan allows the plants, to a certain degree, to dictate where, and in what strength, they should appear. 'They make the decisions,' she says, and their decision is often to self-seed with abandon; her instinct is then to leave well alone rather than banishing the upstarts to the compost heap, a philosophy that may bring a certain anarchy but also a raffish charm to her colour schemes.

Below: painterly colour in the border is achieved with a palette that ranges from deep orange to yellow, with such plants as helenium, echinacea, crocosmia and canna.

Behind these first splashes of painterly colour, bamboo has been planted which arches over as in a secret garden, and which will eventually grow upwards and across to make a wall, thus separating the first from the second area. This second area is in strong contrast to the welcoming cheerfulness of the perennial borders. Designed specifically as a quiet zone, it is part shade and part sun, centred round a bench, a perfect sitting spot, flanked by two tall chimney pots that serve as elongated planters and are filled with tumbling soft grey and ice blue *Teucrium* 'Regale'.

Beyond this calm space, solitude evolves into society, for the third area in this always surprising garden is the space designed for eating and conversation – essential garden activities in Susan's view. Here the ground is paved, and a table waits for food and drink. Plants grow through the gravel in a leisurely sort of way. As far as the conversation goes, Susan has ensured that – for the sake of privacy – nothing can be overheard; on the far wall are two stepped pools served by two chunky tap-like spouts, one above the other, out of which water gushes as if from New York fire hydrants. Behind this aqueous babble all secrets remain forever safe. Decorative old clapboard reclaimed by Susan, once bright green, but now a gentle rural sort of colour makes a fitting background to the urban waterfall.

Following pages: Looking back towards the house, a gravel path meanders through the lush borders, making the garden seem much larger than it is in reality.

51

Left: the double-spouted water feature designed by Susan Collier.: Two simple spouts pour water into two small stepped pools; behind are pieces of decorative old clapboard reclaimed by Susan, which have weathered to a soft pleasing old-garden green.
Right: through the garden along the gravel path, the plants burst with energy, seeding themselves every-where. These are the borders of perennials leading from the house which Susan has planted with two contrasting palettes – on one side soft harmony with blues, lilacs and pinks, and on the other a warm, vibrant combination of sun colours.

Where the garden seems to end, a wall once stood, but now an arch and a beautiful *Cornus capitata* with pale primrose single sepals signals an opening into something else; and passing through you find yourself in a real secret – a completely different garden that runs at right angles across the back of Susan's original garden, as well as of those of several of the neigh-bouring houses. At one end is her studio, from the window of which can be seen, at the far end, a spinney, where the sound of enthusiastic bird song can be heard.

This secret garden has been designated a family garden for children and grandchildren, unstructured with room for games and fun. It is also an experi-mental and learning garden; in here she is planting oddities – plants that she will watch to see how they develop. 'I'm an amateur – I bought the garden and now I'm learning to be a gardener – I didn't know I was one.'

And do her early regrets exist still? Possibly not. 'When I'm sitting outside my studio in this part of the garden, I couldn't be happier – there really isn't a happier place to be.'

Paradise Reclaimed

Above: there is something both evocative and charming in the use of a wooden French wine box as a container in which to grow shallots.
Right: a winding gravel path leads past raised beds made from old railway sleepers, and meanders through a verdant planting of semi-tropical trees and shrubs.
Following pages: a raised pool is made from roof slates found in a skip. Retrieved containers for olive oil are used to grow plants in. The brick party wall has been painted a warm green that seems to make the garden wider.

*I*n the north of London, beyond the street-smart purlieus of Hampstead and Primrose Hill, out to where the hills are high and the streets are green, there are still untouched islands that are very much as London once was. Adam Caplin lives in one of these villages, Highbury, in a quiet street, in a small house with a small garden, that should by rights be like any other, but is actually a total surprise – not only to the viewer, but one feels, quite often to the owner himself.

In this small patch – about 50 feet long by 20 feet wide (15 metres by 6 metres) – and overhung with lowering London trees, railway sleepers sit by olive oil tin planters, real tomatoes grow out of tomato cans and frogs croak in a pond made from discarded roof slates. It all combines to make a design of great charm and originality.

It is not surprising when you consider it that a gardener should be passionate about recycling bits and pieces, junk, industrial off-casts, *objets trouvés*. After all, the whole idea of growing plants, seedlings, cuttings, indeed everything to do with the growth and of a garden, is the very definition of what natural recycling is about.

Adam Caplin takes his recycling very seriously – his entire garden is a series of collages, montages and tableaux, made up of pieces from other times and places. Like so many gardeners, he is an artist, painter and writer. Like so many artists, he is also a man of passion.

'Contrary to what is often thought, I believe that the English are passionate people; it is just that their passion goes into plants rather then into other, more obvious things. Personally I am also a passionate skip hunter – or a "dumpster diver" as they are known in America.'

Like so many ingrained habits, it all started when he was a child – or at least, his father started it. 'He was a very creative gardener and loved finding and creating things, and skips were a natural treasure trove. From him came my love of using all things found to create something new.'

Above: Several pieces of semi-industrial sculpture in the garden convey the idea of an industrial landscape overtaken by nature, a theme which continues throughout the garden. Right: every sort of container is used to grow plants, from painted tin cans to old wooden boxes. Sometimes Adam Caplin chooses appropriate containers for the particular plant, such as these aubergines grown in a can that once held Greek olive oil.

As you peer into the garden from the back door of his house, an immediate example presents itself – a stainless steel sink sitting on an old-fashioned sewing machine base: what could it be? Why, a barbecue of course.

The starting point of any garden is in a sense obvious – it is what you have now and how it becomes what you want to have; the art, of course, comes in marrying the two. 'It's important to remember that we don't live in paradise; everyone, for example, wants to screen something when they have a town garden, and you should plan your garden around that fact.' In this garden he already had some reasonably large trees which helped to screen off next door – and in any event he is in favour of large things: 'In a small garden, too many small things can make it seem busy, confused and even smaller.'

Adam feels that a garden should reflect its owner in the same way that an interior does. A garden that leads out of the house or is seen directly from the house should be partly integrated – the colour inside might reflect the colour outside, and at the very least should be harmonious.

Harmony is important to an artist, and as an artist, he constantly searches for new avenues to explore. 'I've always enjoyed the lateral mind, and the garden became a good place for me to experiment with objects which were made for one purpose and then used for another; ecologically of course, this is also a good plan.' Reflection rather than contrast is the idea – 'too much of that dazzles the eye; it's

not for me.' For the sake of harmony, he even pours different streams of gravel into paths through the garden, and he changes the gravel often, in order to enjoy the different colours and textures.

Like many other artists, he is also concerned – and intrigued – by the use of letters and words on the objects that he finds and recycles into garden pieces.

'Words can be very evocative: a wine box, for example, which is labelled "Chateau Something", is very grounding – it leads to reflection on the box's past life, on its present relationship with the garden.'

Another theme was edible plants grown in food containers, which is actually all about contrast. 'Sometimes it's good to have tomatoes growing out of tomato tins.'

When he started on this garden, the first thing that he did was to strip away all the parts which he deemed unnecessary; and after the stripping away comes the renewal. 'I built raised beds made from skip wood, and a pool near the house was made from roof slates found, of course, in a skip. I designed and made a sculpture which consisted of an upright railway sleeper, hung with chains bought from a crane shop. The idea was an industrial landscape, but one that was being taken over by nature. "Nature will return" was the underlying theme.'

He loves plants in the abstract – the bark of *Hydrangea petiolaris*, for example, or a bamboo with its sculptural form and movement and sound. 'You do find plants that seem to work anywhere, like nasturtiums: – their tumbling foliage is incredibly attractive.'

Appropriate plants, like the tolerant nasturtium, are what he seeks, and like many sensitive gardeners, he wrestles with the idea of horticultural freedom – freedom for the plants, that is, although he realizes that – as in the real world – too much freedom means that the garden will disintegrate. He therefore instils a little judicious integration where necessary. 'You learn to look at plants in a different way, and you learn to experiment. An unchanging garden would be dull indeed and would be somehow missing the point. The freedom that the garden creates is that in many ways you can eliminate the conventional. You don't need a pond or grass – all you actually need is a good starting point.'

Unsurprisingly, this philosophy results in a distinct feel of the country about Adam Caplin's London garden – but it is the real country rather than the manicured version, the sort of country where gardens just evolve with time and love rather than get made.

Hidden in the Wood

Above: at one side of the terrace, water tumbles into two stepped pools; the area is planted with woodland and moisture-loving plants. Right: looking down from the house, across the brick-paved octagonal terrace, through the deep, naturally planted area to the hedged lawn beyond. Following pages: Looking back towards the house from the lawn, surrounded by a clipped yew hedge. The path is framed by two low stone urns and Pyrus salicifolia *'Pendula'.*

*T*he secret gardens of childhood memory – rambling, green and magical places, where every turn seems to bring another pleasurable surprise – are not often found in London, mainly because city gardens are, on the whole, simply not large enough to allow for the unforeseen. But much of St John's Wood, an area to the north-west of the centre of London, was laid out in the early 1800s, in what was then still a rural area and at a time when space – for the wealthy, at least – was a luxury that could be bought. As a result many of the houses in St John's Wood do have large gardens, including the one pictured here by Theo and Renee Laub.

Actually, to call this garden large is an understatement; it is probably nearly 200 feet (60 metres) long and at least 50 feet (15 metres) wide, giving much scope to a passionate and indefatigable gardener like Renee.

The garden was originally owned and landscaped by the well-known garden designer Arabella Lennox-Boyd. Renee, a plantswoman and garden designer, wanted to put her own stamp onto the existing design. She began by adding to the back of the house a conservatory, which leads onto an octagonal terrace, reflecting the shape of the bay that projects from the back of the house. To create the conservatory and terrace, the ground was excavated to basement level, and the result is a sunny sheltered spot, surrounded by deep, stepped octagonal beds that rise above the terrace to ground level.

On one side of the terrace, water, like a moorland stream, cascades over stones into two pools, one lower than the other; above the water, ferns unfurl in a woodland area filled with hostas, decorative, delicate acers and a magnolia stellata that soars upwards. On the other side of the terrace, the stepped beds are planted to give colour and interest in both spring and summer. There are bulbs of course, of every description, and shiny-leafed

camellias; along the base of the wall grow cyclamen and hellebore, and clematis of many varieties.

From the sunken terrace, shallow steps, lined with terracotta pots planted with standard fuschias, one of Renee's passions, and underplanted with annuals like lobelia, lead upwards away from the house. At the top of the steps, two enormous Victorian terracotta pots hold weeping crab apple trees which come together forming an arch.

From here, a narrow, winding stone path leads through shrubs and trees – an area of planting which could hardly be described as 'borders', for what London borders are nearly 20 feet (6 metres) deep? The space is more like an open shrubbery interspersed with planting – like the clematis varieties trained over wooden pyramid frames and the many fuschias trained as standards. In fact, wherever you look there are standardized shrubs – including relatively unlikely candidates such as lilac and *Elaeagnus* and even a *Hydrangea grandiflora*.

Renee explains, 'The original garden was formal – an effect achieved through landscaping. I wanted it to be less so and I wanted to add structure through the plants rather than through hard landscaping – hence my love of standard plants.' There is also at least one fuschia grown as tall as a small tree, warmly encouraged by Renee – 'I love the bark of these larger fuschias, and I keep them properly pruned and under-plant them.'

The winding path ends in a large circular lawn, made even larger by Renee, encircled and enclosed by low hedges of clipped yew, with an arbour at either side framed with pots. At the far end of the lawn is another arbour covered with roses, purposely built low so that it can be seen in a direct axis from the house. Here an antique heavily carved stone font, surrounded by the large-leaved yellow, variegated *Hosta* 'Frances Williams', acts as a focal point, an eye-catcher seen from the entrance to the lawn. In the centre of the lawn, two very old peaches cut right back to their basic outlines are used as frames for climbing roses. A pair of corkscrew willows are silhouetted against the sky with the sun shining through their translucent leaves and twisted branches. It is sheltered here and warm, a place of rest and relaxation. Behind the lawn, stretching to the wall, is a children's paradise – a wild area of tall trees, long grass, camellias and hiding places – the sort of thing rarely seen in London.

All in all, Renee is pleased with her efforts. 'It is a year round garden which is what I wanted, and the dense planting makes it feel country-like.' It is also true that the whole design somehow gives you room to breathe – and that, in London, is a rare treat.

Left: a conservatory and terrace were built on to the back of the house, the octagonal terrace reflecting the bay above it. The raised beds surrounding the sitting area give a feeling of enclosure and luxuriant planting, emphasized by the many pots on the terrace and the steps. Above: a garden for all seasons and all ages. Some parts are planted almost artlessly, with native woodland plants like foxglove and honeysuckle allowed to grow freely where they will.

Left: a sign of good garden design – when an arrangement or a planting, such as this small sculpture of a female figure surrounded by woodland plants, looks as though it had always been thus. Right: At the far side of the lawn is a low arbour, deliberately designed so that it can be seen from the house in a straight axis. In it is an antique Gothic stone font. Hydrangeas arch behind it, and in front of it grows the yellow variegated Hosta *'Frances Williams'; a pair of matching urns frame the set piece, a classic eye-catcher. Behind the arbour is the wild part of the garden where long grass rules and camellias flower in early spring.*

Outdoor Rooms

Green Rooms

Anthony Collett, a well known and very successful interior designer, lives in a solid 19th century house near Shepherd's Bush in West London which he bought from the local council some twenty years ago, after the resident squatters had been evicted. When people say that a garden they have taken on was once 'a real tip', they usually mean that it was a bit of a mess. When Anthony uses the same phrase, he is telling no more than the unvarnished truth – for his garden really was a tip – a dump for everything from mattresses to fridges, and bottles, bottles, bottles – all hidden from immediate gaze by what Anthony describes as a 'duvet of Morning Glory' (*Ipomea*) that rambled and waved over the chaos beneath.

Previous pages: looking down the garden, over tall clipped hedges and the Magnolia grandiflora *to the shrubbery beyond. The strict geometric design gives shape and form in which planting can be more loosely interpreted.*
Above: Wisteria floribunda *hangs from a pergola close to the house.*
Right: the curves of a wrought-iron gate leading to the shrubbery, with a central sunflower motif, contrast with the otherwise disciplined lines of the garden design.

Once he had removed this domestic detritus, Anthony was looking at that most desirable of things for a gardener – and indeed for an interior designer – a blank canvas, empty save for a 'magical pear tree in the far corner.' Because of this, and because the garden was long and straight, he decided to divide the rectangle he saw into four distinct sections divided horizontally by green hedges.

The first area was directly outside the dining room windows. This was to become a broad terrace paved with golden York stone. From there a boundary of green-painted trellis with a gate – 'originally put in to keep the dogs out' – led into the next 'room', a lawn: 'a necessity; we had young children.' The dogs have grown, as have the children, but the gate remains, like a lychgate into a flowered churchyard.

Within the lawn area, borders on either side are disciplined to a degree – the beds are planted with one species only: sedum, whose pinky-red flowers are in bloom almost throughout the year and which are prevented from spilling over by small woven hurdles, anchored along the length of the beds. 'I went through a herbaceous phase and filled these borders with different herbaceous plants but it drove me nuts, so I decided that one species – sedum – was the answer. It suits

me, and it flowers nearly all year round.' From this you will perceive that Anthony is a disciplined man, for whom order and logic are watchwords which apply as much to his garden as to his professional life.

From the lawn, clipped green columns then lead into the third 'room', which he originally planted as an orchard with apples, cherries, pears and plums down each side, planted in a geometric way – not espaliered, but clipped and evenly placed. Unfortunately, several years ago a storm brought down the original, inspirational pear tree, and as it fell it took many of the new orchard trees with it. Order had been sacrificed, so Anthony decided to take out the other trees, and instead planted four *Magnolia grandiflora* in huge tubs: 'I accessorized them with objects and pots. The four trees anchor the space, and the pots around the base of the tubs are planted with white bearded iris in spring, followed by white lilies, and lastly, white geraniums.'

The fourth and last 'room' of this minutely thought out garden leads to the wall at the end. 'This is the shrubbery,' proclaims Anthony, although it must be said that it is a far cry from the sort of shrubbery that springs to mind – it is a word more often used to describe an area filled with heavy-leaved rhododendron and tired spotted laurel. Anthony's interpretation, however, is altogether different: here there are mostly evergreen flowering shrubs like *Choisya* and *Viburnum*, that flower in early summer. 'In May it is wonderful, but it's a two-week hit and then it's gone.' The interesting thing about this space is that the quite densely planted shrubs are not left to follow their natural plant forms but instead are clipped into mounds of different shapes and sizes so that the whole area looks like a seascape of rolling green waves.

Then about ten years ago he was given the opportunity to buy the back half of the garden next door. So, what was once four rooms has now become six. In line with the orchard area he has built a studio, 'a waterproof room, if you like.' And this leads – in line with the shrubbery – into a small, final garden room originally designed as a planting garden for his children and dramatized with a fine, classical Wendy house against the far wall, flanked by garden storage rooms.

Nothing could be further from the informal school of English gardening, but it is a design triumph. 'It is axial and geometric, but in the best of ways, I think. I have very few species, and that suits me. There is little colour – apart from the pink sedum. Almost everything else is white, which works well with the foliage.'

At this point we are walking back through the garden past a small group of *Amelanchier canadensis*, planted beside one of the fences, their leaves just starting to turn a wonderful pale red-gold. As I comment on their beautiful colours, he looks at them with slight suspicion. 'They do have white flowers in the spring,' he says reassuringly.

Above: the design of this garden means that every angle is a secret. Here the high, clipped hedge leads the eye into a garden room furnished with table and chairs.
Left: Originally planted by Anthony Collett as an ornamental orchard, this area is now home to four Magnolia grandiflora grown in huge terracotta containers, and covered with pebbles. Pots around the containers are presently planted with a spring planting of white pelargonium, and bluebells grow in profusion.

Left: one of the four Magnolia
grandiflora, *coupled with*
terracotta containers with Iris
'Elizabeth Poldark'. *A door*
leads into another garden
room, this one inside and
originally part of the next-
door garden, bought by
Anthony Collett and
incorporated into his
existing space.
Right: looking out from the
interior garden room into
the exterior garden room,
where the walls are not of
plaster, but of privet.

Thinking Space

Hampstead Garden Suburb in North London is a unique experiment in suburban living. Founded in 1907 by Dame Henrietta Barnett, it is one of the most complete and finest examples of early 20th century domestic architecture and town planning. Wide roads cross the area (a minimum width of 50 feet/15 metres was one of the original planning stipulations), all trees are protected, and the houses are divided from each other by hedges, trellis or fencing rather than by walls. This gives a remarkable, almost rural, feeling to the whole area.

When the owners bought the house in this idealistic suburban zone, some eighteen years ago, the garden outside was as traditional as you might expect – it sported a rockery, a lawn and a patio.

Above: Leading from the living room is the first garden space – a decked area with room to sit, cook and eat. The decking then becomes a path, leading away past the ancient olive and through grasses and Sedum to the standing stone.
Right: the garden is dominated by the social area, a low dry-stone wall spiral, designed to bring to mind an ammonite, and which seems to lead the eye into the other garden rooms.

Designer Julie Toll was commissioned as a leaving present to the owner by the garden centre group with whom she had worked for eighteen years. Since leaving she has run an alternative therapy practice which focuses on Zero Balancing – a way to bring energy and structure into equilibrium; she has also studied geology, which has given her a keen interest in stone, and she was keen to incorporate both these passions into the new garden. There were also some practical requirements, including somewhere to cook and eat outside as well as a meditative area.

It was agreed that the garden should be loosely divided into four garden rooms, the first of which leads out of the sitting room onto an area of decking which copies the design of the floor inside the house. Here is a barbecue and room for sitting and eating with benches on golden stone, beneath a beautiful maple, and a fine magnolia. It is a private sun trap – so sunny that they planted an ancient olive tree, rescued from a building development in Spain; it is a wonderful specimen, living a pampered life, with the vulnerable trunk and base wrapped in fleece from autumn to spring.

From here the decking subtly becomes a walkway projecting outwards past waving grasses and a mysterious standing stone, made from golden cauxite and

found in West Donegal. The walkway is like a promenade projecting out to sea, and the grasses, waves: 'I love the way that it draws you out and along.' From here, stepping stones take you into a contemplative area – the second room. Here there are rocks – 'ancient ones, Lewisian Gneiss, which is a metamorphic rock from north-west Scotland, and one of the oldest in the British Isles.' They have been carefully placed among pebbles and the space planted with different grasses, half-hiding a minimal sculpture by Carlos Mata, which is surrounded in the early summer by massed iris.

In contrast, a section of lawn leads dramatically across to the third area, which was designed for socializing. The structure consists of a slate spiral wall, low enough to sit on, and made in the traditional drystone manner with a message and crystals hidden in its depths. Formed in the shape of a giant ammonite, with only the top layer of slate cemented together, it is illuminated at night by a hidden uplighter, and was built on site from sacks of Welsh slate lifted over the hedge by crane. It is very simple and very beautiful.

The fourth area is that always difficult space – the front garden. In this case it is the area on the other side of the front door, which becomes a woodland space with acers and azaleas, and plants edged in box add structure and tie it in to the rest of the garden.

The main structural elements of the garden – like the standing stone and the slate spiral – are the features around which the rest of the garden organizes itself. These and other important features like the magnolia and the olive are lit, and the lesser living elements ebb and flow around them according to the seasons. 'The garden has a crescendo of growth. It becomes very lush, and then drops back, and in December and January I feel it sits quietly, waiting – just like the living thing it is.'

Left: the contemplative area, with ancient rocks placed amongst asters, Sedum *and* Miscanthus sinensis *'Morning Light'. The minimalist sculpture is by Carlos Mata.*

Above: around the standing stone are planted Stipa tenacissima *and* Sedum. *The decking walkway leads back to the house.*

Following pages: the spiral is not only a dramatic, sculptural statement, it is also an inviting place to sit, particularly as it is illuminated at night by an up-lighter hidden in its depths.

Theatre in the Jungle

Whilst many areas of London seem to have a village-like atmosphere, Barnes, on the river, to the south-west of London is the real thing. Self-contained and independent, it boasts a bustling High Street, a common, and even a village duck pond – in many ways, though so close to the centre, it does not seem to be part of the greater city at all.

Ian St John lives in one of the many leafy, lazy streets surrounding the village centre. His garden today is an interesting combination of structure and unusual planting: it is not large – about 40 feet by 30 feet (12 by 9 metres), rectangular in shape, and is surrounded by, and backs onto, others of similar dimensions. What is striking is that unlike many other gardens of this size, the basic traditional, rectangular shape has neither been altered nor disguised – in fact it has been used as the basis for the whole geometric structure of the design.

'I began this garden because my late sister had been a landscape gardener and I am a very keen plantsman, and we had always meant to do something together. I am very interested in design but not good at doing it myself, and in this garden there was a distinct lack of structure which I found very frustrating. In about 1999, a friend suggested that I meet the designer, Christopher Masson. We got on – which is very important – and even more important he liked much of what I had done with the garden; I had a lot of exotic plants, but planted in a very random manner.'

As well as wanting to bring more form to the garden itself, Ian also had practical considerations to be taken into account. The fashion for loft conversions is in full swing in this part of town – all around him the houses were getting taller and taller, and he was becoming more and more overlooked. So he wanted privacy, but also, of course, enough light to enjoy the garden.

After Christopher had made his first visit, no word was heard for some time, until one morning a drawing arrived in the post. This showed the garden with a single tree – a cork oak – as a focal point, and a pergola structure. It was not

what Ian had expected, but it gave a starting point on something they could develop together – 'He's so enthusiastic about it all , and good at the big picture whereas I am good at detail; as we worked together I would embellish his ideas – with the pergola, for example, we went from what was originally designed as a flat-topped structure to something that was more rounded and dome-like, and he drew up cross-shaped steel posts, which I prefer to square topmasts, and then crowned them with finials.'

The garden was constructed in phases – the first phase being to put the basic structure into place, which included the first part of the York stone and brick terrace, some sound trellis, and planting the first trees and shrubs. Then came phase two – 'We were both slightly dissatisfied with the design as it was, but couldn't quite work out why until we realized that we needed more height, so we built a raised level at the far end of the garden to give an illusion of depth, and added rendered columns, crowned with urns, to give a more dramatic effect.' And indeed, the raised area, framed by the lofty columns, gives an impression of a verdant outdoor theatre, the columns a proscenium arch, the raised platform the stage.

This theatrical illusion is heightened by the deliberate use, elsewhere in the garden, of overscaled objects, such as the tall square rusted metal planters on either side of the kitchen doors, the smaller column with a succulent-filled urn on top, and around the corner of the house, three big planters standing on pebbles. 'It has been a revelation to me, putting huge things in a tiny garden; there's a lot of very big stuff, but oddly, it doesn't look too much.'

Privacy was enhanced by the deliberate pruning of the trees and taller shrubs: 'It is important to cut and prune in the right way; Christopher is very good at creating strong shapes, whilst I am more cautious about deep pruning. At the back of the garden I cut everything in a very flat way so that the height is there but it isn't too bushy, this giving a roof, but light underneath. I am keen not to lose the structure of each plant.'

The lawn has always been a bit of a problem. 'It doesn't really like being here, which makes it a constant struggle; we laid cobbles around the edges because the verges are so bad and there needed to be a point where the lawn stopped and the borders began; actually what started as a practical idea, has actually become a part of the design, fitting in well with the stone and brick throughout the garden.'

His exotic plants are wildly happy – the *Clianthus* with its vivid red bunched flowers in bunches, the *Melianthus* shooting upwards and the *Tetrapanax*, which sometimes flowers in the depth of winter – in fact the whole garden with its combination of airy structure and galloping plants could possibly – with not too giant a stretch of the imagination – be a corner of a lost city somewhere in the South American jungle, rather than somewhere in Barnes village, S.W.13.

Left: Theatricality and structure are added to the garden with the inclusion of a striking column supporting an urn planted with Astelia, *which leads the eye upwards to the foliage above.*
Above: on a low brick pier at the side of the garden, a patinated metal container is planted with agave.

Tropical North London

Above: a suitably exotic elephant figure amongst the sub-tropical plants of Declan Buckley's garden.
Right: a tree fern dominates the morning terrace; beyond is the pool crossed by a plank bridge which leads to the dense planting beyond.
Following pages: The pool, nearly as wide as the garden itself, forms an effective break between the paved terrace and the slate-chip path leading to the exotic part of the garden where Euphorbia mellifera, *bamboo and loquat thrive.*

From Declan Buckley's raised ground floor window, all that can be seen of his garden is a verdant canopy of tropical exotica waving softly in the wind, a sea of spreading tree-fern fronds, the green propellers of the banana palm and the flicking tongues of bamboo leaves. Obviously no ordinary garden, this tropical haven is in fact set in most urban North London, all noise and bustle, and practically next door to the grounds of even noisier Arsenal football club.

Amazingly, the whole garden is only five years old. When Declan, a garden designer, moved in, it was 'a blank canvas; that is to say, it was like a thousand other London gardens – a forsythia, rambling roses, two old lilacs and a concrete terrace.'

The flat he was buying consisted of the ground floor plus the basement and its garden, and while he was waiting for the completion of the sale, he passed the time by designing the garden. 'This meant that when I eventually moved in, I was ready to go with a lot of the initial planting; it was doing things backwards really, but it worked.'

He knew that he wanted to design a garden that veered geographically towards the tropics, 'one that I could look at out of the window in the winter and not feel depressed. I come from the south of Ireland where the climate is very mild and you can grow all sorts of species; I have also lived in San Francisco, and spent time in New Zealand and north-east Asia, where I had seen many wonderful exotic gardens, so I knew you could do something. I had also noticed that in the centre of London, many shrubs and trees consistently exceed the suggested final size – indeed some things seem to grow almost twice as large The ground is, of course, often warm here, which means that what you can grow in a central city garden is quite different even from what you can grow in a suburban garden, never mind in the countryside.'

The dimensions of the garden are typical of many London gardens, measuring about 20 feet by 75 feet (6 by 23 metres) – narrow, but relatively long,

and divided by an area of exotic woodland planting into two open areas – one next to the house which catches the morning sun, and the other, a paved and raised area at the far end of the garden which captures the evening light. Between the house terrace and the woodland planting is a wide rectangular pool, almost the width of the garden and edged with stone. Broad planks form a bridge across it and its width both subtly and naturally divides the garden, whilst making the whole garden look broader and larger.

This house is five storeys high, and having previously had a flat with a roof terrace, Declan felt very exposed, so much of his initial planting was done in order to gain some privacy, and many of the shrubs and trees were grown for their vertical effect. The slow-growing tree ferns are tall enough to stand under now; there is at least one banana tree that is 15 feet (4.5 metres) high, and still growing, as well as a rice paper plant (which at Kew Gardens is grown in the hothouse) running rampant, and an exotic fruit tree, the loquat, which is soon to bear fruit. Exotic plants like good drainage, so they are actively helped by the rubble-filled soil which makes up part of most London gardens.

As well as making the garden a private place, Declan also wants to bring the whole garden up to the window level of the raised ground floor, and indeed the canopy, after five years, seems, from the kitchen window, almost close enough to touch. And of course the design of the garden has also changed in other ways. 'I started with filler plants, which I then took out as everything began to grow. From a full garden, you start cutting back, and over the years, it has begun to consolidate into an altogether simpler garden.'

As luck would have it, it is raining when I walk out into the garden. Beneath the roof of palms, ferns and bamboo, I walk along the slate chip paths, with the sound of the rain falling softly somewhere above; at that moment, it is not hard to imagine that one is in a tropical rain forest some-where, particularly as when I get to the glass door leading into the lower level of the flat, there, immediately outside the door, beneath a particularly solid canopy of vines and climbers, Declan has installed that mainstay of all the most luxurious safaris, an up-to-date, fully automatic hot, outdoor shower. Welcome to the tropics of London.

Above: At the far end of the garden, a suitably exotic Eastern parasol gives shade to a table and chairs; beyond, a raised terrace catches the afternoon sun, and white Iris confusa, *bamboo and* Phormium *grow nearby.*
Left: the height of the trees and shrubs can be judged, in this view from the balcony, by the fact that the brightly coloured parasol is almost obscured by the dense foliage.

The Smallest Garden

Above: a metal grille set in a false wall contains bamboo. Right: seen from inside, the outer decking mimics the floor; the roof slides back to enhance the outdoor feeling. A series of cut-out shapes echo the design of the interior. Seats fold out, exposing mirror panels behind.

The success of a garden is not judged by its size – which is fortunate, since this successful roof garden measures a mere 13 feet by 6½ feet (4 by 2 metres) – and is definitely the smallest garden in the book. It is on the upper level of a mews house in West London; mews houses were traditionally built for grooms, with the stables below and living quarters above. Today, although the horses are long gone, cars have generally taken their place, so most mews are still arranged with domestic life on the upper floors.

Because the space here is so small, the garden designer Paul Cooper realized that in order to succeed it should be seen – quite literally – as a continuation of the room which opens on to it, which is a contemporary living room, with a glass and steel roof that architect Alan Crawford designed to slide back to half its depth so that the two areas can – and do – become one open space.

On all levels, this internal/external integration was encouraged. The boards of the living room floor are echoed by the decking outside, and the colour of the inside walls is echoed by the colour of the textured finish of the outer walls. Even the design of one living room wall, where the flat-screen television, CD system and fireplace set into square voids cut out of the wall, are mirrored in the cut-out squares on the corresponding wall of the terrace, which form frames for an original and effective water feature.

The fact that this garden is on a roof meant, of course, that all the components must weigh as little as possible; Paul Cooper therefore decided to construct a false wall, about a foot (30 centimetres) away from the existing wall – inside which all the necessary elements could be attached.

This new 'wall' was made of marine ply, and coated with a flexible, American textural paint – widely used in the US as a coating for clapboard houses, as it is pliable, tough and flexible, and hides a number of ills. It does have drawbacks though: 'Although it looks good, it wasn't actually that easy to apply; we did it in very hot weather and the texture became extremely sticky and difficult to manipulate.'

A water feature has been designed within three cut-out squares in the new, false wall; each square is filled with narrow, vertical strips of glass, and each strip given a nibbled, rough edge. Over these water cascades, and as it does, the rough glass breaks the flow, giving the falling stream movement and sparkling life.

Above: a glass brick wall that maximizes light reaching the roof garden while preserving privacy at the same time. Clematis is trained across it.

Left: on the wall that faces the interior, the central element is a water design that descends from the top, through two cut-out spaces; each space is filled with vertical strips of roughened glass over which the water runs, its movement broken by the irregular edges.

More glass was added to the garden in the form of a glass block wall; mews houses are by definition built closely together, and the garden was obviously overlooked, so on one side, the glass block wall gives necessary privacy without restricting any equally necessary daylight.

The garden had to be easy to look after – the owner is not a plantsman and didn't want to bother with much maintenance. So three niches and enclosures hold plants, mainly bamboo and grasses, which are kept in place not with ties or stakes but with narrow metal bars that give the effect of cages or grilles: 'I liked the idea of containing living things within cages.' Beside these cages are horizontal metal rods which hold and train climbing plants.

Along one wall are steel-framed slate seats, backed with mirror, which fold out from the wall. To go with the seats is an ingenious arrangement whereby a ring set into the of the wooden deck may be pulled up to reveal a rectangular eating table. Also set into the wall are mysterious small circular discs, each about 8 inches (20 centimetres) in diameter; these are loudspeakers, an extension of the audio system installed inside the house.

Paul describes this miniature space as less of a garden and more of an integrated 'interior-scape'. 'A lot of what I do now, particularly in London, is a cross between garden and interior design; as space becomes more restricted, the alternative to a conventional garden or terrace has to be considered.'

He is also known for his intelligent and imaginative use of lighting, and in this tiny space he has installed not only uplighting in the plant cages as well as behind the cascade, but also three lights set into the wooden deck flooring. The effect is of being inside a warm and welcoming bowl of light.

Classical

After the Snow

Previous pages: in this timeless English garden, a peaceful spot has been designed with a pebble pond, flanked by clipped Pittosporum tenuifolium *'Tom Thumb',* Euphorbia characias wulfenii *and* Alchemilla mollis.
Above: in front of the garden bench is a stone mosaic, designed by Gay Wilson to represent compass points. Right: beneath the surface of the pond the water mechanism is housed out of sight; the pool itself is filled with pebbles, making it safer for small children to play nearby.

Wimbledon, over the river to the south-west, is one of London's villages, today hidden beneath a confusing web of one-way traffic systems, new town centres and railway lines. But behind it all still lies the original village with quiet leafy roads and large detached houses, all with gardens to match.

Gay Gray's house is set back from the street and with a view from the drawing room of a green and flowered, peaceful garden, full of interesting and unusual plants and trees, easily reached through the kitchen door. But it wasn't always the haven of planted peace that it is now.

'We have lived here for thirty years and brought up four children, so for many years this garden was geared to them. It was a classic rectangular garden then – a family garden divided by a shrubbery toward the rear, behind which were all the things necessary to children's garden life – where they could play and hide, with sand pits and other necessities.

'I had always thought of it as a small garden, but one morning, I woke up to find the garden under snow, and suddenly I realized, seeing the garden in its white-blanketed pristine state, that it was actually a large garden, and it made me think what I might do with it.'

They began by making the lawn area circular where once it had been rectangular, figuring correctly that this would make the lawn itself appear wider. But then Gay's husband, an architect, began work on a long-planned new kitchen which dug somewhat into the garden area, so they realized that a master plan was needed, and probably professional advice too.

Enter garden designer Gay Wilson. 'I felt that I was a beginner still, and knew that Gay could help – and she did. She came up with the garden that I would have created; we wanted water, seating and a secret garden – she brought it all together, and her planting schemes were lovely.' The architect in the family wanted an all-white garden, while Gay Gray had been hoping for colour. The compromise, and a very successful one, is a garden designed in a pale palette – white, yes, but also pale pink, lavender and lilac, as well as soft-toned foliage.

The new design was made five years ago, and
today looks as mature and settled as though it had
been in place for the thirty years of the Grays'
tenure. The whole garden is a pleasing contrast
between the discipline of structure, and the fullness
of the planting.

Because the new kitchen has a rounded D-end,
they were able to build a broad terrace that encompasses it. At the other side, against the boundary, is
a wide pergola, with dining table and chairs. To
cover it they planted a vine for leaves and shade
which has been so successful that it produces
grapes, on which the happy pigeons gorge. Near the
house grows a very healthy *Solanum jasminoides*
'Album' which flowers from Easter to November.

The circular lawn area leads to a charming
round pebble pool, the perfect answer to the always
difficult combination of (grand-) children and
water. Although the pool is deep enough to house
the mechanism, it is filled with pebbles so that the
water is very shallow, and therefore safe; around it
is planted *Alchemilla*, white poppies and salvia, a cool haven on a hot day.

To one side of the pool, against the boundary, is a garden shed where once a
rose arbour stood. A good example of what can be done with seemingly
unpromising material, this structure was, surprisingly, bought ready-made. But
with the boards painted in a soft grey-blue, and laden with climbing roses, it now
looks more like a hidden, secret tiny cottage than a everyday old garden shed.

Flowering trees are everywhere: on one side of the garden is a camellia, an
apple, a lilac and a winter flowering *Prunus autumnalis*; at the far end is a soar-
ing mimosa tree – *Acacia dealbata* – which also flowers in winter.

Separated from the pool by a short path, lined with box and lavender, is a
bench that faces the house, in front of which is a stone mosaic designed by Gay
Wilson in the form of a star or compass points.

Behind the bench, two wooden arches, one set on either side, further divide
the space; but because the area between the arches is clear, the sightline is unim-
peded, and the eye is taken further back to the end of the garden where an
Elaeagnus and the yellow-leaved *Choisya* 'Sundance' have been planted to give
a splash of brightness in dark winter days.

This quiet area furthest from the house, and complete with table and chair,
has now become somewhere where, in her own turn, Gay, should she so choose,
can hide from the demands of others.

Classical Mayfair Elegance

Above: along one side of this narrow enclosed garden, George Carter has placed standard Cupressus amazonica *between oak benches; although not the same as the planting on the other side of the garden, the clipped trees echo the espaliered hornbeams and maintain the formal outline.*

Right: the narrow rills or canals are designed to make the garden appear longer and to reflect any available light; they are edged in pale Portland stone, a traditional material used in classical design.

There can be no such thing as a garden which is not a challenge either in design or horticultural terms, but designing a garden in a confined space, which is much-overlooked by tall buildings, certainly presents a very trying challenge; happily it is one to which designer George Carter, known for his formal garden designs, rises with aplomb.

The garden in question is in Mayfair, in the heart of central London, and serves a tall, narrow classical building which has been converted into flats – not an ideal site for a garden. It was, says George, 'basically just a large light well.' Most of the flats do not have access to the garden, so it had to be as attractive to look at from a height of six storeys as it was at ground level. The garden was also to be designed as part of a group of three other buildings in the apartment complex, and it is designed to be seen both as a separate garden as well as being viewed, on occasion, as part of the greater whole, to which end doorways and pedimented door cases have been designed to allow access and views from one garden to another.

In these circumstances, the clear-cut lines of the classical, formal garden, popular since the 17th century, seemed the obvious route to follow: 'That is often the thing with town gardens, they need something architectural and something visual. When designing a classical garden, it is important to relate the axes of the garden to the architecture of the house, and this can often be done with water.'

The practice of using what were originally drainage canals for ornamental and design purposes, relating to the house had already been established in France by the 16th century, and was elevated to a state of near-perfection by the great André Le Nôtre in the garden he designed at Vaux-le-Vicomte.

George Carter's garden in Mayfair has two narrow canals or rills in line with the ground floor windows of the building – and, as required, the water uplifts the whole space by reflecting the daylight on a sunny day. Lack of light in the garden was a major problem, and as well as the water, George encouraged and emphasized what light there was by using pale Cotswold gravel and Portland

stone paving around the rills; both acted as reflectors, throwing light back into the darker areas of the garden. As he says, 'Now, even on gloomy days, the light tends to zing about a bit.'

As it can be relatively easily clipped into a smooth wall of leaves, pleached hornbeam has long been a prerequisite of the formal garden. In this garden George has clad the walls to first-floor level with tightly cut and trained hornbeam, which adds interest without masking the other features, and also makes the space greener and less urban. 'We also put in another, unclipped, hornbeam at the end of the garden; it gives height and has an impact on all three gardens.'

The planting was designed to be effective all year round, and rather than flowers, herbaceous plants and foliage were used with small, topiary box plants and *Viburnum tinus* planted in pots.

Another classical principle of garden design is to use repeat elements in order to emphasize the length, so here, on a miniature scale, George has done just that. As well as the hornbeam on one side, on the other are a series of small oak benches and standard *Cupressus arizonica* at intervals between them.

Between the two windows stands an urn on a column, echoed at the other end of the garden by two obelisks which flank the pedimented doorway, and which act as a focal point; both they and the doorway are underscaled to add to the illusion of length, and both the urn and the door surround have been designed to echo the architectural decoration on the street-side of the building, another classical trick.

The whole garden has been discreetly lit from the bottom upwards – for George Carter is adamant that you should never use artificial lighting to try and emulate daylight; the glow of evening light is far preferable, and by lighting from below, you can create interesting shadows which complement the architecture of the garden. Other advantages include the fact that other gardens are not disturbed by the light and also, in a block of flats, the garden is more often seen by night.

George was able to work closely with Gavin Johnson-Stewart, the interior designer of the complex – something that is not always possible. 'He used an interior palette of washed-out stones and greys, so I was able to reflect a lot of that in the garden tones and the colour we used for materials. I think that that has helped to give the garden a softness and harmony that it might not otherwise have had.' That, and the discipline of a trained classical eye.

Left: looking away from the building, the eye is drawn to the doorway framed with a pair of classical obelisks; the doorway, which can be opened into the garden beyond, is in line with the urn pictured on the previous page.
Above: a view across the canals at the far end of the garden highlights the pleached hornbeam (Carpinus betulus) that runs the length of the party wall; uplighters are used both around the trees and in the canals.

An Open Book

Above: the front garden is designed with a formal clipped box parterre enclosing the blossoms of Rosa 'Elizabeth of Glamis'. Right: along the back wall of the rear garden, white Rosa 'Climbing Iceberg' and deep-coloured Rosa 'Veilchenblau' form a rich screen. Following pages: looking towards the house, the combination of formal garden structure and exuberant planting with rhododendron, Rosa 'Dark Lady' and Rosa 'Tour de Malakoff' is the result of careful planning.

The area known as Little Venice is so called because of the canal which winds its way through it. It is a picturesque area of quite startling contrasts, with fine, stucco Regency houses overlooking the brightly painted and decorated narrow boats moored along the edges of the canal, each community living in its own, very different world.

This garden is larger than average for London, since the owners acquired the neighbouring basement flat and its garden some years ago. Surrounded by mature trees, it was an ideal space in which to create something wonderful, and in this they were ably helped by garden designer Susanne Blair, who had previously worked with them on an earlier garden.

The new, extended space was an open, empty book and fittingly they decided to make each side of the garden – old and new – reflect the other: 'Like a book, rather than a mirror, a book with pages that were similar in shape, if not in every paragraph, and with a central spine – the original wall dividing the properties – the majority of which we retained, in order to break up and give instant structure to what would have otherwise have been too open an area.'

With these basic design principles in mind, it became obvious that the garden should be relatively formal, creating architectural shape and structure with hard landscaping, plants and water, in the form of two pools, fed by a narrow canal or rill. 'We were inspired by the canal in front of the house; I suppose we wanted to have our own small version, right down to the different levels.' The pools are host to fish, including ghost koi, and to a changing display of growing colour; raised pots in the water are planted up for every season, including winter, and lighting is set into the pools to highlight the design.

In formal garden design – as in any good garden design – the structure of the garden reflects the architecture of the building: the owners wanted both front and back gardens to reflect the classical lines of the Regency house. The small front garden is both an introduction to the house and to the larger garden behind – a preface to the book, so to speak; its clean lines complement the

classical structure of the façade overlooking the canal. It is designed as a formal parterre, with box-edged beds that spill over with white roses in the summer.

The back of the house, with its graceful Regency curves, is also reflected in the structure of the garden. Subtle undulations in the swags of trellis along the walls, and in the lines of the raised terrace at the rear of the garden, echo the curve of the raised ground floor balcony. From the box-hedged beds, edged with box and brick paving, come more curves in the form of full, lush colourful planting.

The planting is rich, exuberant and, in a way, almost unexpected. It is this coupled with discipline of the structure that makes the garden so interesting and unusual. The owners love, really love roses, and they are planted everywhere; they also love a particular colour palette that is reminiscent of a *fin-de-siècle*, *La Traviata* floral arrangement: shades that range from tones of grape and wine, from the deepest of dusky burgundies and brown-red clarets, through purple-reds, black-reds and softer blue pinks. There are swathes of *Agapanthus*

and red and pink hydrangeas, dark pink-purple penstemon, *Papaver* 'Patty's Plum', *Campanula* 'Elizabeth', and of course roses everywhere, including 'The Prince', 'Tradescant' and 'William Lobb' – most of them from old rose specialist David Austin, and all as fragrant as possible.

Yet for all this exuberant bounty, the garden is, oddly enough, according to the owners, quite low maintenance. 'We have used a combination of mediums – York stone, brick and gravel – which are easy to look after, although, if I were to do it over again, I think we would use a different, finer shingle. It is so sheltered that even in the autumn you can sit outside, and in winter it is wonderful, because there is so much formal structure, emphasized by the box hedges and the clipped box balls. And the lighting has been designed for winter as well as summer, placed particularly to highlight the structural elements.'

For all its formality, this is a calm, quiet garden; and as if to prove the point, as we stand there admiring it, a kestrel, so rare in central London, lands on the lawn and walks unhurriedly to the pool to drink. A secret garden indeed.

Left: a composition in claret, including the oriental poppy, Papaver orientale, 'Patty's Plum', and Rosa 'William Lobb'. Rosa 'Tradescant', Rosa 'Tour de Malakoff' and Rosa 'Sombreuil' can also be seen. Below: the structure of the garden is disciplined; the borders are edged with box and steps lead up to the upper terrace, guarded by a pair of stone lions.

Left: Looking down from the house the structure of the garden can be seen along with the central wall – the imagined 'spine' of the book. Two rectangular pools are fed by a narrow canal and edged in brick, as is the gravel path and the central lawn. Raised planted pots are set in either side of the pool next to the house.

Above right: in the other 'page' of the imagined book, a seating area is approached through pots of lilies and Rosa 'Tour de Malakoff' tumbling forward onto the path.

Below right: beneath the swagged trellis that runs along the party wall, box-edged borders contain Rosa 'Belle de Crecy' and Rosa 'Tradescant' as well as Hebe 'White Gem'.

West London Restored

Above: a structural garden of great simplicity, anchored by decking which not only forms a dining area, but which also acts as a walkway connecting each part of the garden.
Right: in front of fine original Victorian iron railings, Kim Whatmore has planted a combination of texture and soft colours, including Digitalis x mertonensis, Phoenix canariensis *and* Acer griseum.

*O*ne of the things that is noticeable about city gardens is that there is sometimes no correspondence between the house and its garden, and indeed the style of the garden may even be in complete opposition to that of the house. This house in West London is period in style, dating from about 1840, but the owners are of a contemporary thinking, designing the interior in pared-down fashion; the garden, happily, follows the same understanding as the house.

At the rear of the house, the stucco façade is embellished with wonderful wrought-iron railings that lead down beside steps from the house into the garden; at the far side of the lawn there is a door which leads into what used to be quite common 150 years ago but is rare now, a mews house belonging to the main house, which opens into the cobbled alley beyond the wall. This means that the garden itself is a completely hidden box, surrounded on all three sides by walls.

At first sight, the garden space seems almost period in its green simplicity; but then you notice that this simplicity has not been brought about by the passing of time, but the editing of an existing space, the introduction of a new simplicity, to match the mood of the house.

It has not always been thus: when garden designer Kim Whatmore first saw the garden, about three years ago, it had really been let go: 'It was really, really overgrown, with bamboo everywhere – basically it was a forest. From the quality of some of the existing shrubs and trees, I realized it was a garden that somebody had originally taken a lot of trouble with, but that was long ago. My brief from the owners was to design the garden to work for them, and they had two specific requests: one was how to make the garden user-friendly for their small children, which meant keeping the lawn – always remarkably difficult in London; and the other was that they wanted to connect the main house with the mews house, both visually and spatially.'

Apart from these two specifications, Kim Whatmore was given what must be every gardener's dream – completely free rein with the design. She was allowed to do whatever she liked, as long as she remembered the mantra – children, lawn and mews.

The answer to connecting the two buildings at either side of the garden was to use deck boarding; but instead of a single terrace or path, Kim made a giant two-sided picture frame of the decking, running it as a path parallel to the house and, at right-angles, as a broad eating terrace that also leads down the length of the garden to connect with the mews house door. Edged in brick, the decking both frames the lawn and gives a place from which to view the restful planting around the walls. 'Decking can often look too smooth, particularly when it is used in large quantities, so I used ridged and grooved boards that add texture, as well as making it all a bit softer and a bit more contemporary.'

Once Kim had cleared and cut back the existing tangle of shrubs, she found that there were several shrubs and trees which would soon look very good again. 'There was a bank of camellias, and a huge magnolia, as well as a mountain ash, a mulberry and a fig. I was thrilled because they were all mature and made a fantastic background to the garden.'

But having existing, established plants can also present problems: 'First of all the trees do make the garden dark; secondly, when established plants are already present, and you have to add new things into a depleted border, it is very difficult to connect the existing plants with the new ones – there is such a difference in size and maturity, and any connection has to be in scale. Another problem is that established plants tend to take any nutrients in the soil.'

When a garden is a square and the all-important lawn is in the centre, the structure of the borders becomes even more important. Kim has designed them to be predominantly green, which is both restful and means that things can thrive even without much sun. There are tree ferns and acanthus, large-leafed plants that demand attention; and scattered amongst these dark patches are bright candelabra of foxgloves and fuschias that light up the space with megawatt brilliance.

It's like a textile design: 'For the border closest to the house, I was inspired by the ornate iron railings; they reminded me of one of those train stations that you see in the south of France, where exotic plants are planted through the railings that back the platforms.'

Now, only in its second year of planting, the garden already has a mature, settled air about it; the new plants connect with the established ones, and there is a rhythm and a balance in the borders, all set off by the soft grey tones of the surrounding wood. It is indeed a restful and pleasant place and one that quite brilliantly makes a virtue out of necessity.

Left: the view from the mews house back towards the house. The original iron railings were an integral part of the design, coupled with the need to have a large area of lawn. The boards used for the decking are ridged rather than smooth to add textural interest to the area.

Terraces

Floating Gardens

Previous pages: these moored barges are home to a variety of shrubs and trees that grow on the very roof tops. Above: an infinite variety of plants and shrubs grow in these flat-topped barge gardens, ranging from perennials like asters and annuals like nasturtiums, to sturdier contenders such as crab apple and quince trees. Right: the gardens are connected by boardwalks, which are communal and open to all; across the five barges seating has been designed to enjoy the waterside views.

Nick and Juliet Lacey live in a rambling apartment in one of the old wharves on the River Thames, looking across the river to the City of London and upstream to the neo-Gothic spires of Tower Bridge. Since the gradual closure of the old docks, many of the grain warehouses and wharves on the south-east bank have been successfully converted into individual working and living spaces surrounded by galleries, shops and restaurants, and today the whole river area jumps with life.

The Laceys, whose apartment is on the fourth floor of their wharf, are numbered amongst the earliest of residents having lived there for nearly thirty years. They do not plan to leave: 'well, only by our boots,' says Juliet. Some years ago Nick, an architect, bought the moorings immediately outside the building, and began to convert the barges tied up there into comfortable living spaces; as they gazed down from their eyrie onto the moored barges, it became obvious to them that the long flat-topped boats would make wonderful floating gardens – roofs on the river, so to speak. Verdant barges are, after all, hardly a new idea – Dutch barges, traditionally, nearly always had flowers and vegetables growing – albeit in pots rather than on the boat itself.

First contender for the green experiment was the barge nearest to their bird's-eye view: 'We didn't know what would happen. What could we plant? And would anything grow?' To find out, they installed large metal containers on top of the barges, and then brought in the earth by lorry which they then dropped by crane around the containers. Each container is only about a spit deep and they knew that much feeding of soil and watering would have to be done.

It worked: plants grew – and grew, and grew. Five years on, these river follies number four; the latest one is still a planting in progress. The first garden – the one planted five years ago – is now well-established and the others are following fast behind. Shrubs include *Choisya*, *Hebe* – varieties of

which wink at you from every walkway – as well as rosemary and other aromatics; there are climbers like honeysuckle and clematis and night-scented *Nicotiana*. London rocket – originally introduced by the Romans – is self-seeding, as are the bountiful nasturtiums. The rampant success of all this happy plant life encouraged Julia to add some trees, and the four gardens now boast between them weeping ash and robinia as well as – most charming of all – fruit trees like quince and crab apple. Interestingly, following the self-survival instinct that plants have, some shrubs have begun to miniaturize: the several buddleias, for example, have all developed smaller panicles than they would normally sport.

Wooden boardwalks run the length of the gardens, and Juliet has lately introduced that most civilized of garden features – small sitting areas from which one can marvel at close quarters the diversity of river life. A small table for picnics or drinks, complete with chairs, and overhung by a quince tree sits at the water's edge. What could be nicer or more in keeping with this aqueous fantasy?

Those who get to enjoy these waterfront amenities at close hand are the residents of the living spaces below the gardens, who number about seventy in total. They are an interesting mixture – some who work in the arts, some who work in the city (complete with pin-striped suits) and a smattering of families, complete with babies (and one granny).

Looking down from the apartment balcony today, the effect below is of a tapestry – not the tapestry of a formal knot garden, but more the effect of a leafy green verdure. This is due mostly to Juliet's own taste: 'My taste is for a sort of messy muddle of green, a jungle effect, combined with a lot of colour so that they could be clearly seen from shore.'

The birds of the river have taken to these floating gardens too. 'There are ducks and geese. The Canada geese and the greylags are a bit of a hazard in the spring – they come looking for places to nest and stump over everything with their enormous feet, but I love them really and they make lovely nests.' A flock passes over by at that moment and she hails them fondly. And then there is the resident pair of wagtails, the odd crested grebe and, of course, a now ubiquitous heron. One bargee is a bird-lover who works to protect the eggs and babies from the predatory magpies and crows that also haunt the area, although other garden birds have yet to spend much time there – perhaps the two resident cats, who have eliminated the rodent problem, have seen to that.

So the gardens have been a resounding success – acknowledged by the fact that they won first prize for a community garden in a borough horticultural competition. Ironically, though, the same council that has honoured them is also threatening to move the barges on, thus destroying the very gardens they have praised. Garden lovers everywhere will be hoping they do not succeed.

Left: few London gardens can have such a fine view of Tower Bridge. Lavender grows along the boardwalks and over the skylights.

Above: the contrast between the fragile plant life of the gardens and surrounding industrial architecture, both of the old wharves and the uncompromising shape of the moored barges, gives this project its charm.

Following pages: as well as chosen plants such as rosemary, several species have seeded themselves, including London rocket, introduced by the Romans, and buddleia, known for its hardiness.

North Terrace,
South Terrace

A roof terrace garden can be many things, but never a traditional ground-level garden with all the gardening conventions that implies. This roof terrace – or rather these roof terraces – are part of an apartment bought by a couple who no longer wanted the responsibility and space that a whole house entailed. Their children grown up, they decided to find a contemporary apartment and completely change their way of living, and part of that change was to give up their much loved garden.

The apartment that they chose is in a light-filled modern block in the north of the city, high above one of London's canals. The terraces flank both north and south sides of the apartment, and from inside the apartment both of them can be seen from every angle. This meant that it was very important that they should both look interesting all year round, and so garden designer Declan Buckley was asked to ensure that this would be the case.

'There was no getting away from it – in other houses you can ignore the garden in the winter, but not here; and so it was a lesson in adapting the design to the surroundings. Because of their orientation, each terrace is very different, and required very different planting, and yet because they can both be seen together, they needed to have a coherence. The terraces are shallow, they are exposed – they are in fact, difficult.'

The weather at the top of these buildings is not forgiving either: it is windy, hot and cold – to survive extremes of weather all the planting had to be wind-resistant, shallow-rooted and grown in planters that would be secure.

Inside the apartment is a dramatic curved staircase and Declan decided to design planters that were of the same dimensions and lines as the staircase so that there would be a strong and immediate visual link between the interior and exterior. They are also very large – oversized in fact – but they work much better with these shallow terraces than lots of small-sized pots, which would have been dwarfed by their surroundings.

Far left: on the terrace which catches the sun, simple large pots hold sun-loving plants including Icelandic poppies and Eucomis bicolor.

Left and below: specially designed containers hold plants that can survive rooftop exposure: Verbena bonariensis, Agapanthus *and* Festuca glauca.

Above: the view over the canal is striking and ever changing; it was necessary that the planting be equally striking, as well as relatively weather-proof and easy to maintain. Right: this balcony is now sheltered enough to hold a table and chairs, and Phormium *and grasses grow happily in their large containers.*

Above right: the inside of the apartment is decorated in simple contemporary style with a central curved staircase linking two storeys. Designer Declan Buckley wanted the exterior to complement this modern simplicity with 'architectural' plants and curved planters that followed the lines of the stairs.

The owners' last garden had been planted with favourite shrubs and plants like magnolia, camellia and hellebore, all of which they would have liked to bring to the new terraces, or at least to plant some similar varieties; but Declan was having none of it. 'They wouldn't last two minutes up here; we needed things like coastal plants which are used to extreme conditions; although there is an irrigation system, the rooftops dry out so fast, and plants become pot-bound, sun-baked and blow-dried.'

On the southern, sunny terrace, desert plants do well; on the northern side, facing both north-east and north-west, he has planted tough things like *Phormium*, mountain flax, and *Pittosporum*: 'It gives height and copes better than bamboo on a roof like this. It drops its leaves and won't get blown to pieces.' There is some colour on this side – *Geranium palmatum* with its big blowsy pink flowers, orange *Crocosmia*, red-hot pokers and iris. There are grasses, too, which are tough and sturdy and take on warm tones in the autumn.

On the other side of the apartment, the southern aspect sports an altogether sunnier face: in full desert mode, a silver-bladed *Aloe vera* and fat cacti all look very much at home; cape daisies, nasturtium, agapanthus, allium and verbena all thrive in their pebbled pots. And at night, clever lighting highlights the strong shapes of plants and planters, adding interest within the apartment.

'The important thing about a roof landscape,' explains Declan, 'is that it isn't real, in the way that a natural landscape is, but it can and should be made to relate to the real thing. The way I have planted these two terraces mean that they work with the wider landscape and the view beyond. There is a difference, but there is also a relationship.'

A Provençal Terrace

Above: an olive tree, grasses, lavender and other plants usually happier growing in the Provençal hills rather than in North London. Right: decking covers the terrace, except for a border of gravel around the edge of the garden, to prevent small children from going too close to the outer wall. Canvas 'sails' cover the area directly outside the living room door.

O f course you can't really have a small pocket of Provence transposed to a terrace somewhere in North London, but there is nothing wrong with importing some of the key elements, particularly when you happen to have a terrace which is so sheltered that it can be too hot to sit out on during the average English summer.

The flat itself is reached along an outside corridor. Inside, a flight of stairs leads into a bright living room and from there out into a sky-high terrace, today sunny and warm with, surprisingly, in one corner what appear to be full-rigged sails, white and unfurled against the sun.

The owners, who have a young family now aged four and one, have owned the flat for about seven years. 'We'll never move,' they say, 'particularly now that the terrace is so perfect.' They realized that they would have to do something when the original concrete terrace floor became so hot that they were unable to go outside; that, coupled with the arrival of their soon-to-be toddlers, meant that action was necessary. The sun is with them all day from its rising to its setting and the sitting room doors are open from April onwards. Happily, they are not overlooked – although the flat is not especially high, they are above most of the other relatively low-level buildings in the area.

The first thing to do was to paint the deeply unattractive red brick outer walls in a neutral shade. The next task was the floor: 'We wanted to deck it, but beyond that fairly basic requirement, we couldn't think of how to arrange the other important thing on a sunny terrace – how to get flexible shade without it costing too much. Luckily we spoke to the decking company about our problem and they recommended us to John Hall of the garden design company "Gardens and Beyond"; we told him what we were looking for and he showed us these triangular sails – which had the added bonus of being very cheap, which was good, as the decking certainly was not!'

So, above the terrace are three, elongated triangular, woven sails, which are arranged to overlap slightly. 'We decided to buy ready-made sizes, rather than have them specially made. We designed the layout around the existing structure of the terrace, the sails, and the way that the sun moved around during the day, which of course affected their positioning and meant that they had to be one end of the terrace rather than the other. 'So they are situated directly outside the sitting room door, which has the added advantage of making the shaded area a

direct extension of inside. In fact the whole terrace is an extension of the interior: 'During the summer months, the doors are open and everything moves out there including the children and the toys, which meant that something else had to be resolved – the question of safety.' So – in a simple and effective move – they made a toddler no-go area, a border directly under the wall, finished with pebbles and sand. They lit the borders with small, coloured polystyrene, stone-like lights that blend in with the pebbles in a very realistic way.

In these beds, as everywhere else on the terrace, are hot weather plants that positively flourish in this happy place – provençal classics and wonderful grasses which grow to almost wild proportions: 'They are just beautiful; I didn't know they were going to grow this tall, and I positively love them.' And loved, too, are the lavender, herbs, like oregano, and perennials like *Achillea* and *Verbena*. Sturdy trellis on the apartment side of the building supports colourful climbers like passion flower and clematis.

'We wanted a garden that would be low maintenance and also fairly wild and free – hence the lavender and herbs. It's also very windy up here so they also had to be quite hardy – just like in the hills of Provence; we use a combination of shallow planters and a watering system – we literally don't do anything.'

Of course, no self-respecting provençal garden would be complete without an olive tree, so why should a London terrace be any different? Here, an olive stands proudly in a metal container; to date they have already harvested olives – one black, one green.

A table and chairs sit at one end of the terrace; the London Eye fills a tiny corner of the skyline. Life is sweet here in N.W. Provence.

A Piece of Sky

*I*t is not often that you meet a Londoner who has completely changed his or her way of life and moved from one side of the city to another; for although the distances involved may be relatively small, such a move is life-changing, so many are the differences between one spot and another. Michèle Osborne however, who is French by birth, has done just that, moving two years ago from the slopes of Notting Hill north of the river to the plains of Elephant and Castle in the south, where she now lives in a lofty apartment built in a converted telephone exchange – an apartment which came with its own flat roof space, reached by a staircase.

A garden designer by profession, Michèle sees the move as 'a complete liberation. In Notting Hill I had a small shady garden – here I have a garden that is almost in the clouds.' Designing, as she does, terrace and roof gardens for other people, made her feel that she wanted to do something with her own personal little patch of sky.

Fortunately, the roof of the old semi-industrial telephone exchange was made of large concrete slabs, so she knew there would be no problem with weight; she was more concerned with getting a certain simplicity of design: 'It doesn't work in a roof garden to have too many things going on; the skyline should not compete with the planting.' Although her particular roof space is not particularly large – approximately 30 feet by 16 feet (9 by 5 metres) – she wanted to use two different materials – iroko wooden decking, which mellows to a silvery grey, and slate, to divide the space, and add some ground-level interest. The design centres round a broad octagon of iroko, with an iroko boardwalk leading away and making a connection between different areas of the roof. The whole roof area – which encompasses other gardens, many of them now designed by Michèle – had been divided by the developers with cross-grid metal screens. In a chain of DIY supermarkets, Michèle found a hazel brush fence, sold by the roll. She installed it behind the metal screen so that the cross-grid shows through. 'I wanted to be able to see the combination of metal and hazel – to use the hazel to hide the screen would have been too fussy for me, and not in keeping with the urban scenery.'

Left: birch trees have been planted in large containers where they thrive. Cosmos, Alchemilla mollis and Phormium make a pleasing, gentle contrast.

To tone with the wooden decking, she decided to have planters in silver-grey metallic tones and she installed four oversized ones, each holding two birch trees. 'I was resistant at first to the idea of birches, but then I saw that they thrived.' Indeed, they look perfectly placed with their silvery bark and delicate leaves silhouetted against the skyline.

There can be few places in London where in a direct sight-line are two such contrasting landmarks – the spire of a beautiful early 19th century church designed by John Soane, and the fabulous 20th century 'Gherkin', the curved and banded Swiss Re headquarters, designed by Norman Foster, and fast becoming one of London's better-loved new buildings. 'It is an incredible view. You see such a vast expanse of sky and you become so aware of the city – so much more so than when I was living at ground level.'

More steel bins are planted with lavender – 'greys and silvers, that come

alive when the lavender flowers' – and different grasses: 'I didn't want too many grasses but they so love being here. And I am able to have hostas, because at this level, there are no slugs!' There are succulents in pots which have been semi-sunk into beds of pebbles, different varieties of herbs, and even, scattered around, some pumpkins. In many ways, it resembles a garden built on the edge of the sea. Michèle has purposely avoided adding too many other colours: 'I tried having other annuals, but it didn't really work. There is so much going on at this level and I don't really feel like competing – the sunsets are incredible and so is the sky.'

As Michèle has designed other gardens for the same building, there is now a continuity of design which is pleasing, and she spends a lot of time up on the roof. She really does feel that hers is a secret garden: 'I am very lucky. It doesn't feel high up here, it just feels very privileged.'

In a shallow, raised gravel bed and in containers, succulents such as Echeveria, Sedum, Sempervivum and Cacti are planted at a level where they can best be appreciated and enjoyed.

145

Clerkenwell Pavilion

Above: from the pavilion, doors open on several sides onto this terrace which enjoys regular use, year round.
Right: a view of one of the seating areas of the terrace, where decking and Scottish river pebbles form a textural base for shrubs and trees including eucalyptus and bamboo.

To build a garden that is the only outdoor space for a family with several energetic young children, and which is situated on top of a block that consists mainly of offices and studios, does not, on the face of it, seem like a terribly good idea. But for designer Fiona Naylor and her family, this large roof terrace garden has been an unqualified success for all concerned.

Their apartment is on the top of a building in Clerkenwell on the edge of the City of London, and it is a particularly urban space, with a clanking industrial lift connecting offices, warehouses and the domestic penthouse on the top floor.

'When we bought the apartment, it was just one large floor with a flat roof above. We decided to build upwards into the centre of the roof space; we wanted to build a sort of all-purpose living pavilion, and we then thought that we might use the remaining roof space to make a garden around the pavilion.'

Fiona is a designer and therefore this idea did not intimidate her as much as it might have others. She even blithely opined that, with the help of a crane, they might sort out the garden completely over three or four weekends. As it turned out, the easy part of that was actually the crane hire – like many things in life, once you know how to do it, it is not as difficult as it seems. The harder part, however, was the time scale. Instead of the optimistic four weekends, it actually took an entire summer of weekends, but it was, at least, a very productive summer.

As a professional she had a clear idea of what was needed. 'I had the concept, I knew what I wanted to achieve, and I worked with Lindsey Whitelaw at Whitelaw Turkington on the sort of plants and planting that would work within my concept.'

The new pavilion, a glassy, light-filled box, was designed to open directly onto the terrace. 'The secret of a garden or terrace is to move seamlessly from the inside to the outside – if you have to go up a staircase it loses something; there should be no effort.'

Left: a working terrace is what Fiona Naylor wanted and the herb border, planted a round a skylight includes healthy specimens of rosemary, chives, mint and fennel, all sheltered by a thick hedge of Elaeagnus.

Left: looking through the glass door, it is, at first glance, hard to accept that this is a roof terrace in central London. A rill runs between river pebbles; trees and shrubs including bamboo, birch and corkscrew willows, thrive in the rarefied air. Following pages: on the sunny side contemporary steamer chairs look out across the decking to the sylvan landscape in the sky; a haven of calm, peace and quiet.

It helps, too, that, even with the new building, the remaining outside area was large enough to design with confidence. 'It was a question of balance. I wanted something that was quite sculptured so that it would seem to be an extension of the building, so I wanted to create defined areas within the open space.'

As a garden it works really well; as a roof terrace – or several – it is outstanding. It consists of two huge terraces with walkways between, and divides easily into rooms. The west terrace is a sitting area, and the south-facing terrace is another, specifically used in the mornings; at the other end is an eating area, complete with built-in barbecue. It is very secluded; ivy climbs some of the walls and *Elaeagnus* forms an evergreen barrier: 'We are overlooked so it was important to have some sort of screen. It had to be good for children and tearing around, as well as for us to use; we incorporated a sandpit and a little bit of water, which is brilliant. I wanted it to be reasonably low maintenance and there is surprising little weeding – weeds just don't seem to get up this high.'

What really strikes you when you walk around the garden is the presence of trees: mature and healthy birch trees – four of them – twisted corkscrew willows, and soft grey-green eucalyptus, as well as bamboo. Out of the pavilion, decking leads to a deep bed of Scottish river pebbles in which are rows of bamboo and the two corkscrew willows; rosemary, lavender and other herbs grow in abundance. 'The herb garden is important for me. I wanted the garden to be somewhere where we could actually grow things and use them.' Interestingly the trees are planted not in soil but in a lightweight growing medium, which retains moisture much better than soil; they feed it which is why perhaps the garden has developed its own eco-system – over the years that they have been there, snails and other such things have arrived. 'Now we've probably got as many snails as in an earth-bound garden.'

They wanted somewhere that they could enjoy for as much of the year as possible – and enjoy from inside when the weather is bad. 'I feel we need more colour change and I am thinking of planting a beech or some tree that gives colour in other seasons; also perhaps some annuals. It's still evolving, which is what I like about it, and I love the garden all the more for having done it ourselves.'

Prairie Rose Garden

As in any great city, there are many ways in which London can be seen and enjoyed. There is the London that is seen at street-level – all architecture and city life – and there is a green, eye-level London with its vast collection of trees in every park and garden. Thirdly, least obvious perhaps but ubiquitous never the less, there is bird's-eye London – a London of a thousand different aerial views from terraces and roof gardens, a London of familiar landmarks seen literally in a different light.

Gail Thorson and Tim Macklem are Canadian and came to live in Highbury, North London, some six years ago. Although they were looking for a flat, they needed, unsurprisingly, some outdoor space – not as much as they might have had in Canada,

Above: dining table and chairs seen through some of the container-planted grasses that wave across this roof terrace.
Right: colour is a vital component on this terrace: the metal railings leading up are painted a dark red, while walls are painted chrome yellow and terracotta red. Galvanized containers give a dramatic effect, and are planted with equally dramatic grasses and vivid Verbena.

perhaps, but definitely somewhere outside to which they could repair. A top-floor apartment in a new building provided a possible solution: the interior was light and airy, and outside a small open well led up a metal staircase to a large roof space, already laid out by the original architect and affording plenty of space in which to sit – and indeed to garden. Although the garden was not badly laid out, after a while they began to hanker after the wide landscapes of home. On a visit to the Chelsea Flower Show, they saw a medal-winning garden by noted designer Christopher Bradley-Hole; they liked everything about it – it was both simple and very contemporary. Bradley-Hole was commissioned and slowly – very slowly – a design began to take shape.

'It took ages for it to happen – a small garden often does. Our brief to him was not very explicit: it was "How can we solve this?" We didn't say that we wanted it to be low maintenance or anything like that but obviously the design had to incorporate species that would flourish in both wind and sun, for as in all roof gardens, weather conditions beneath the sky are more extreme and pronounced than when encountered at ground level.'

Many people would have opted for a garden in the Mediterranean style, 'all yuccas and so on, but we didn't want that; what we wanted was to use pines

Far left: the roof top is covered with two surfaces, decking and gravel; a sky-light opens between a set of galvanized containers planted with clipped box, against the terracotta red side wall.
Left: a container full of Agapanthus africanus silhouetted against the deep red wall.
Below left: memories of the Canadian prairies. Galvanized containers planted with waving grasses that sound almost like the real thing as the wind blows through them; a large trough contains herbs and Verbena bonariensis.
Right: sitting on this bench surrounded by grasses and hardy plants evokes memories of sitting out on a jetty by the water.

and grasses to remind us of the Canadian prairies – in miniature, of course.'

Within the initial design structure, colour played a simple but vital part. The wall behind the staircase to the roof was painted a vibrant blue, and on the roof itself one wall was painted a strong terracotta, another a rich chrome yellow.

The roof surface is covered in two materials – cedar decking and loose gravel – and a wooden bench is put against one wall. It is an evocative place: 'For us, the cedar decking is the dock on a jetty, and the stones around are the water. We love to sit here.'

Around the perimeter, a row of the precisely shaped Japanese pine – *Pinus parviflora* – form a screen, and in galvanized metal planters of different sizes are huge clumps of rustling grasses – the true prairie grass, of course – *Panicum virgatum*, and other species including, *Miscanthus sinensis*, 'Autumn Light', which flowers in late summer. There is clear reference to, and indeed, reminders of the rolling prairie plains.

It is so sheltered that it is often too hot to sit there in the day, but supper is eaten when the sun goes down. A contented olive tree sits in a large pot, along with different varieties of iris – many bought over the internet. *Agapanthus africanus* and a wisteria languidly clambers up. They spend so much time up here that they are thinking now of adding a small pavilion. It is a perfect spot: you wouldn't know, sitting there in the sun with the whispering grasses all around you, that this was a London rooftop and not the Canadian prairie – well perhaps you would, but gardens are all about fantasy, after all.

Contemporary

The Enchanted Kingdom

Previous page: a winding path leads through a garden that pleases both children and adults with its fantasy landscape. Above: the rough grey slate path winds away through grass mounds, like a river flowing through the hills.

*E*aling is in many ways a typical leafy west London suburb – it is only a couple of miles out of the centre, but it seems to exist in a place and time all of its own. Large redbrick houses, built in the 19th century for solid comfort, stand quietly in their own large front and back gardens.

Sunil and Leslie Wickremeratne asked Laara Copley-Smith to design their garden. But it was not to be just any garden – they have three children and the original brief was to create a garden that would be a pleasure for adults to sit in and enjoy, but would also be a kind of magic kingdom for children, where fantasy and imagination would be partners and nothing would be quite as it seemed. Features would include mountains, a ravine, doubling as a long winding road, and enchanted follies – not quite what you would expect to find in an average suburban garden.

Although unusual, this was not, particularly complicated, to begin with, but as it gathered momentum, it turned into a far more complex scheme. The house itself led, as do so many of its type and age, straight out from the back rooms onto a rectangular area of block paving. Beyond that was little else but lawn with 'things like *Choisya* and periwinkle – all the sort of things that you would except to find in Ealing,' says Laara. A bonus was the presence of a few established trees, mainly old apples and pears, with beautiful gnarled and curved branches and trunks.

The rectangular house terrace was very dull, so naturally Laara re-laid it, giving it curves where there were straight lines, and designing it to lead down a shallow step to a lower circular area, edged with curved stone seats. In the centre is a low (coffee table-height) cylinder of water, which pours down the sides of the cylinder onto pebbles banked-up on the ground. On the other side of the terrace is another seating area – this time a circular dining table furnished with huge high-backed wooden chairs which, with their exaggerated dimensions, seem to be an integral part of the garden's fairy tale, waiting for some giant-sized, mirth-filled feast.

Below: there is a wonderful brightness and exuberance in this palette, too often rejected in favour of softer shades. This late summer border is alight *with* Pennisetum, Rudbeckia *'Goldsturm'*, Alstroemeria *and* helenium.

Left: Crocosmia *'Amberglow'*.

Stone and water are constant themes throughout the garden. Stone features not only in the form of Welsh slate on the terraces and along the ravine path, but also in the form of standing stones – silent silhouettes, carefully placed where they best set off the shapes and forms of the other elements. Water ripples over rocks and stones, and comes up suddenly amongst the grasses, almost unseen, like a secret spring or stream.

A low wall encloses the paved terrace area and beyond it is a central curving lawn, the edges of which are softened by lush plantings of grasses and shrubs. There is an Eastern influence here, and also sculptural elements; there are low, fountain-like ferns and stately tree ferns, and at the far end of the lawn is box, tight-clipped into mounds, like a bird's-eye view of dark green, rolling sea. Golden and tawny-red acers act as punctuation across the lawn. These, with their distinct foliage and subtle colour variations, are a vital part of the tonality of the garden. The owners had asked for a palette of reds through yellows, oranges and golds – not the easiest colour spectrum to work with, although Laara admits that by the time she had finished the design, she appreciated the variants and tones of the yellow palette in a way she had never done before.

The lawn curves upwards towards what is known as the ravine – a meandering path, which could just as easily be the bed of an ancient, long-dry river. Either side are long curved grass mounds: low from an adult point of view, but easily imaginable, to a child's eye, as a range of hills rolling into the far distance.

The ravine-path leads to the rear of the garden which was once just a wilderness, but now planted as a secret wild garden with shrubs as well as grasses, including *Miscanthus* 'Morning Light' and *Carex elata*, which move and sway in the light.

The lighting in this garden is particularly dramatic, and accentuates the mood of fantasy-fairy tale which is inherent in the design. Clipped and topiarized trees are lit from beneath, as is the circular water table and other mysterious features at the back of the garden, all casting strong shadows and creating pools of light.

Because of the strength of the shapes and the defining lines throughout the garden, it looks good all year round, even in winter. And even in winter, too, the sense of fairy-tale fantasy remains ever-present.

Above: on the terrace outside the house is an oversized wooden table and chairs that work well with the dramatic design of the rest of the garden, bringing a sense of fantasy and storytelling.
Left: the stone-paved, circular terrace leads onto a serpentine lawn, edged with bright mounds of colour, including Imperata cylindrica 'Rubra' *and* Pennisetum alopecuroides. *In the distance, a bonsai-form pine is a striking focal point.*

161

Miniature Marvel

Above: in this small London garden, on the back wall above a raised bed, is a stone bas-relief by William Peers, above a slate a water feature designed by Jill Billington. Right: from the house, the fullest extent of the garden can be seen, and the intricacy of the different levels can be appreciated. The complex water feature tumbles down to basement level.

One of the ways to extend a small London garden – and this garden is certainly small – is to create different levels and clever perspective, a device which works admirably in this small, tree-surrounded Chelsea garden.

When the owner first saw this garden in 1997 it was singularly uninspiring – it wasn't even a garden, but a concreted basement level yard, complete with original outdoor lavatory. As he says, 'Frankly, it was a mess.'

The house, like many others in Chelsea, is a pretty, narrow, white-painted terrace house with the living room on raised-ground floor level, and the back garden reached through the basement, and surrounded on three sides by rather high, dark walls.

'Although I had a large garden in the country and had taught myself something with that, I just didn't know what do with this garden; but I knew Jill Billington and her work and I liked what she had done, so I asked her to come and convert the space into something I could both use and enjoy looking at, using water and as many fragrant shrubs and flowers as possible.'

As well as the garden, there was work to be done on the house itself; the owner wanted to build a new kitchen at basement level across the whole width of the house, taking out the original back wall and extending the kitchen into the existing garden space. To accommodate this plan, the whole garden had to be dug back, which presented an opportunity to raise the far part of the garden to a higher level. Jill designed a small flight of brick steps, leading up towards the back wall and a small upper terrace. As the owner says, 'I wouldn't have be brave enough to put all these stairs into the design, but they work.'

The new kitchen extension also meant that he was able to build out on the raised ground floor, creating a small garden room which opens onto another terrace, also reached through French windows from the ground floor sitting room. A traditional iron spiral staircase curves down to the basement level.

Like many enclosed London gardens, the temperature is extremely mild. On the terrace is a potted lemon tree heavy with yellow fruit which is allowed to stay out all winter, and several clematis, chosen to ensure flowers throughout the season, are planted on the wall behind. A mirrored panel – one of several in the garden – reflects light and gives a feeling of added space.

Far left: the lower pool at basement level is silent and calm, and planted with species that enhance the beauty of the water.
Left: seemingly simple, the planting here is actually subtle and harmonious; around the water feature are planted ferns, clematis and Trachelospermum jasminoides.

Fortuitously, this tiny garden backs onto one of the largest gardens in West London – an 18th-century rectory full of mature and beautiful trees. Jill wanted to use the height of these trees to make this garden appear larger – to use the view rather than to fight against it – and to make the smaller garden appear to merge seamlessly into the treescape behind, using a combination of traditional London garden plants such as clipped box, and lavender to give shape and form.

It is fair to say that there are few gardens which do not benefit from the addition of water: its appearance, its movement and its sound are always pleasant and soothing. In this garden, the water feature or features look larger than they are. On the back wall, beneath a strong focal point – a sculpted stone panel by William Peers – a cascade flows over a slate zigzag, designed by Jill, into a straight-sided pool; the water then appears to flow beneath the upper terrace, re-appearing as a second pool before falling as a flat sheet of water into a final pool on the basement level. In fact both upper and lower cascades and pools are separate runs of water, cleverly designed to appear as one.

Unsurprisingly, the outside lavatory has gone, replaced by a small garden shed fitted tightly into a corner of the upper terrace; like a tiny house, it sports a pointed roof, is painted in a soft neutral tone, and is covered in climbing roses, clematis and jasmine.

The only drawback in this small but perfectly formed garden is the effort needed to keeping it looking groomed. 'It's strange,' admits the owner, 'but it's actually far more work than my much larger garden in the country, because here there is no room for error or mess. In a large garden a certain amount of untidiness can be absorbed into the whole, but in a small one, if there is anything at all out of place – dead leaves, weeds, anything – the whole thing immediately looks a mess.' But this is a small price to pay for miniature perfection.

Above: Town garden herbs including bay and lavender occupy the upper level of the iron spiral staircase.
Following pages: view from the top of the spiral staircase.

Stockwell Garden

Above: the large front garden is planted for a spring display, including Amelanchier and spring bulbs.

Stockwell, in South London, is home to some beautiful and commodious Georgian houses with big gardens; sadly many of them were left untended and unloved for many years, resulting in near dereliction. When this house was bought by its current owners, two doctors with three young children, it was a burnt-out squat. For nearly four years they all camped in the grounds in a series of sheds while the wreck was made into a desirable home.

When the work on the house had been completed, designer Jinny Blom was brought in to make the garden as good as the house. Her brief was relatively straightforward – if a trifle daunting. The owners, who didn't know anything about gardening, wanted something that was easy to maintain. They also wanted somewhere for their children, and their children's friends, to be able to play safely; they wanted to be able to see the children from anywhere in the garden. They also wanted to be able to entertain their own friends.

'The architect had designed a very tall door at the back of the house and a quite small deck in front of it,' says Jinny. 'I think he envisaged the rest of the space as simply garden, but it just wasn't going to work like that; they needed a stronger garden and it is important to have structure in a garden of this size.'

So she began by building a second, larger terrace made of black Indian limestone and, because of the owners' aversion to gardening, she designed at the far side of this terrace two large raised beds, one rectangular, the other square, and filled both with easy-to-look-after plants. The purpose of the beds was twofold: at 18 inches (45 centimetres) high, the broad edges are at sitting height, and Jinny envisaged them as being used in the event of a large party. 'I think you could have lunch for sixty on that terrace now.' Secondly, the planters acted as an architectural break between the children's and adults' spaces.

The beds are planted almost naturalistically – with tall and graceful grasses, and a variety of shrubs. 'The planters were supposed to look like a huge stripe of meadow. All the plants will survive together; they all have about a ten-year lifespan, before you are down to the last three species. Beneath the grasses and shrubs is a layer of assorted and interesting bulbs to give interest over the seasons and I have asked them to leave it until February and then cut everything down, so that it can all re-grow.'

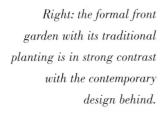

Right: the formal front garden with its traditional planting is in strong contrast with the contemporary design behind.

Below: wide wooden seats, built around two Catalpa bignonioides 'Aurea' that will adopt an umbrella shape with careful pruning.

Left: over-sized raised beds divide the house terrace from the lawn beyond. Perennials such as Verbena bonariensis, Melianthus major *and* Salvia uliginosa *are attractive and easy to maintain. Right: designer Jinny Blom has used decking, paving and grass to delineate different areas of the garden and their different uses.*

Between the planters, Jinny built a 'causeway' of decking to link the terrace with the lawn, and with the gravel on the other side of the planters. The causeway was made to exactly the same dimensions as the over-sized house door, thus bringing the slightly difficult door shape into the overall garden design.

Walking round the other side of the planters you come into a different sort of garden: a large lawn with no borders but instead clumps of bamboo, mimosa, and old mature trees. Three catalpa trees add another element, surrounded by gravel and growing through the centre of three square wooden seats. At night uplighters set into the seats shine into the branches. The trees are meant to be clipped into umbrella shapes so that one day they will form canopies over the seats.

'The bottom of the garden,' says Jinny, 'is a slightly wild area for the kids to play in – roses, geraniums and tough rye grass. The shed that they had used as a kitchen when they were camping here was painted and kept as a relic of those times. Along the back fence, I planted bamboo: no one I have ever heard of has jumped into a bamboo grove – it is incredibly thick and spiky, you run the risk of impaling yourself – so it makes a pretty good security fence.'

In contrast, the north-facing, front garden is planted in a relatively formal manner. 'My personal rule of thumb is that a front garden should always be simple and should not draw a lot of attention to the house. This particular garden is designed to be at its best in spring and has bulbs, spring flowering clematis and *Amelanchier*.'

The look of the garden belies the amount of work that went into the planning of it. 'These small London gardens require so much thought. You have to allow people space to live in, and look at the inevitabilities of daily life, factoring them into the design. It has to be pragmatic and look as it was intended, without being overdone.' And in this she succeeded – with honours.

Waterloo Haven

This small, hidden jewel of a garden designed by Tommaso del Buono and Paul Gazerwitz, is near Waterloo Station. This is frankly a surprise in itself, because at first sight Waterloo is a harsh and quite bleak area of the city, probably best known for its terrible traffic, as well as being the home of the Eurostar and the South Bank Arts complex – altogether an area seemingly devoid of vegetation. Indeed, the street in which this garden is hidden looks more like a mining town in the north of England than a street in a city of gardens. Behind the house, one of many small 19th-century workmen's terraced cottages, a large and ugly block of flats towers over the garden. It was definitely a design challenge, and there was a limited budget.

The brief – for an architect and a fashion editor who, naturally, have very definite ideas on design – was that the tiny garden was to be contemporary, witty and modern. The garden, overlooked by the ugly block of flats, boasted no interesting features, save an outside lavatory – once to be found in gardens all over Britain, now a rare sight indeed. Naturally the owners wanted to keep it.

'The whole garden was pretty derelict,' says Tommaso; 'The first thing we obviously had to do was to create some sort of screen along the back of the garden to hide the intrusive block of flats, and then to use the area in front to create what we hoped would be a tapestry of different colours and textures – a sort of Persian rug effect with a permanent planting, like a horticultural weave, through which different types of plants would flower at different times of year.'

At the back of the house there had been built a tall glass-fronted extension, the height of the house, which at ground-floor level was the kitchen; the owners wanted the part of the garden immediately outside this kitchen to be linked in some way with the new space within. To this end, a long strip of cobbles from their Gloucestershire home had already been laid both in the kitchen and out into the garden. Thus the garden was divided into two distinct parts – the long

Above: a glass fronted kitchen extension opens out into the tiny garden of this small terraced house; the use of the same stone floor surface both inside and out provides continuity and allows the illusion of extending the limited space.
Right: Despite its size, this is an abundant garden; flowers and leaves jostle together, allium, lilies, fig, copper beech. The planting seems luscious and luxuriant.

Left: black bamboo was planted at the back of the garden as a screen. The colour scheme for the garden ranges from mauves and dusky pink to almost black.

174

Below: a silvered panel, created by Pedro da Costa Felguieras, is a dramatic backdrop for the fig tree in front. The outhouse is original and has been retained in the new scheme.

paving which relates to the extension and the rest which lies in front of the original building.

Unusually, but not surprisingly, given the owners' professions, low maintenance was not high on the agenda – it was more important that the colours and styling were right. 'As far as colours and plants were concerned, we all discussed what would work best,' says Tommaso, 'and inspiration came from such diverse things as a piece of paper with a blob of fuschia ink on it – the owner's favourite colour – and a much-loved dress by John Galliano.'

To screen off the offending flats at the back of the garden, Tommaso decided to plant black-stemmed bamboo and surround it with a surface of black slate chippings, forming not only a practical but also a dramatic backdrop for the rest of the garden.

The planting in this confined space is informal within a framework. Rather than little bits of planting, there are distinct 'streams' of plants, where the shape is controlled but the planting itself is very soft and fluid. Tones are dark and strong, with patches of colour and also flashes of gold; peonies, fritillary and iris are the signature plants, all loved by the owners.

'We went for mauves and dusky pinks to stand out in front of the copper – mauve allium and *Papaver* "Patty's Plum"; purple sage, catmint and different geraniums including the moody *G. phaeum*. There was also a wonderful black iris, "Superstition", and even black-leafed cow parsley. The colours had to be worked at and were sometimes vetoed; I also injected a gold element, supplied by some of the grasses and *Achillea*, which I tried to use like gold thread, weaving the brighter strands through the darker ones.'

The next stage took place a year later. 'One of the side walls was covered in ivy. When we took the ivy down, we discovered a very neat recess in the wall behind a fig tree in the corner of the garden. I wanted to bring light into the dark space that was there, so we commissioned a panel [from Pedro da Costa Felguieras, see pp. 26–31] that was in essence a simple piece of marine plywood, clad in silver leaf and then lacquered. The idea was to make a backdrop for the branches of the fig, as well as lighting the whole area under the canopy of the tree.'

What is wonderful about this tiny garden are the long views that you get from the house; from the moment you come in through the front door, the garden can be seen in flashes, with quick snapshots of the scene beyond. The fact that part of the interior and some of the exterior is cobbled with the same paving gives a seamless continuation to the scheme and of course makes everything seem so much larger. It is very self-contained and tranquil in here, and it is hard to believe that but a short distance from this place of peace and quiet, hundreds of trains, throughout the day, busily disgorge thousands of commuters and travellers from Southern England and all over Europe.

Designers

Jill Billington, BA, FSGD
tel: +44 (0) 208 886 0898

Susanne Blair,
Flat 32, 11 Sheldon Square,
London W2 6BQ
tel: +44 (0) 207 359 7427

Jinny Blom Landscape Design,
43 Clerkenwell Road,
London EC1 M5RS
tel: +44 (0) 207 253 2100

Christopher Bradley-Hole
Landscapes,
55 Southwark Street,
London SE1 1RU
tel: +44 (0) 207 357 7666

Declan Buckley,
Buckley Design Associates,
5 Laycock St,
London N1
tel: +44 (0) 207 226 3697

Del Buono Gazerwitz,
1 Leinster Square,
London W2 4PL
tel: +44 (0) 207 243 6006

George Carter,
Silverstone Farm,
North Elmham,
Norfolk NR20 5EX
tel: 01362 668 130

Anthony Collett,
Collett-Zarzycki,
Fernhead Studios,
2b Fernhead Road,
London W9 3ET
tel: +44 (0) 208 969 6967

Paul Cooper,
Ty Bryn,
Old Radnor,
Presteigne,
Powys LD8 2RN
www.paulcooperdesign.co.uk

Laara Copley-Smith,
101 Framleigh Road,
London W7 1NQ
tel: +44 (0) 208 933 1344

Gardens and Beyond,
47 Highgate High Street,
London N6 5JX
tel: +44 (0) 208 340 3409

Todd Longstaffe-Gowan
Landscape Design,
43 Clerkenwell Road,
London EC1M 5RS
tel: +44 (0) 207 253 2100

Christopher Masson,
7 Spencer Road,
London SW18 2SP

Michèle Osborne,
12 The Old Telephone Exchange,
20 Liverpool Grove,
London SE17 2PY
tel: +44 (0) 207 703 1704

Julie Toll Ltd,
Business & Technology Centre,
Bessemer Drive,
Stevenage,
Herts SG1 2DX
tel: 01438 310 095

Kim Whatmore,
156 Dalling Road,
London W6 0EU
tel: +44 (0) 208 741 2994

Gay Wilson,
33 Balmuir Gardens,
London SW15 6NG
tel: +44 (0) 208 788 0931

Page 1
Garden by Pedro da Costa
Felgueiras: see p. 26.

Page 2–3
Garden by Susan Collier: see p. 48.

Page 4–5
Garden by Ann Mollo: see p. 12.

First published in the United Kingdom in 2004
by Thames & Hudson Ltd, 181A High Holborn,
London WC1V 7QX

www.thamesandhudson.com

First published in the United States of America
in 2004 by Thames & Hudson Inc.,
500 Fifth Avenue, New York, New York 10110

© 2004 Editions Flammarion, 2004

British Library Cataloguing-in-Publication Data
A catalogue record for this book is available from
the British Library

Library of Congress Catalog
Card Number 2003115138

ISBN 0-500-51178-0

Printed and bound in France by Pollina : L 93076 b